The Raven's Flight Book of Incense, Oils Potions and Brews

The Raven's Flight Book
of
Incense, Oils,
Potions and Brews

by Raven Womack

Pendraig Publishing, Los Angeles

Pendraig Publishing, Sunland, CA 91040
© Raven Womack 2007. All rights reserved.
Published 2007.
Printed in the United States of America

ISBN 978-0-9796168-1-5

Table of Contents

Introduction

This is not a spell book. This is not a recipe book. This is a book about magickal products. What they are, how they are made, how they are used and how they work. This is a book that I was asked to write. As the owner of Raven's Flight Magickal Apothecary and the main formulator of the Raven's Flight magickal product line, I was asked by some of my customers to write a book on how to use the many products that were available. In mulling over my thoughts for the book it occurred to me that knowing the philosophy and theory behind the products could help the users to gain a whole other level of understanding when it came to actually choosing and using their magickal products. I am firm believer in the philosophy "knowledge is power".

Since this is a book about magickal products, for the sake of clarity, let's define what I am referring to when I say magickal products. Magickal products are mixtures, blends and concoctions made (hopefully) by magickal people to help themselves or others attain specific goals and desires. Magickal products are tools of manifestation. Magickal products can be as simple as two herbs put into a bag and carried around for luck, or they can be complicated matters involving many ingredients and processes to achieve the desired effect. I have tried to cover many of the magickal products available today, but as this is a growing and ever-changing business, I am sure I have left some products out. My apologies for that. I have included at least a brief explanation of all the types of products that I make and some that I don't make but that are available.

Magickal products have been around for millennia as humans have always sought to take advantage of the energies and qualities of different substances to help, heal, soothe, enrich and enamor them or others. In times gone by, every village, town or settlement had at least one practitioner who was adept at concocting these products and most every one knew how to make some sorts of general potions, charms and such. Obviously, times have changed, but there are still those of us who are drawn to the use of natural magick to help them attain our goals. While the village practitioner has been replaced by the metaphysical store and the internet, this age old practice of exchanging currency for potions, lotions, incense, oils and brews still goes on and there are still those among us who believe that magickal products should be authentically made with quality ingredients and real focused intent.

Today, there all sorts of magickal products on the market and in my opinion some are good, some are great and some are crap. Hopefully this book, along with experience and experimentation will help you discern the real stuff from the mass-produced crappola. Of course, I think my products are wonderful and I hope you all buy lots of them, but I have to admit, there are some other really well made and quality products out there as well[1]. I also have to admit that my opinion is not the last word on what's good and what's not good in the realm of magickal products, but I do base my opinions on some pretty solid criteria. There are lines of magickal products out there; no I will not name names, which are of the lowest quality imaginable. These are produced to maximize profit without any concern at all as to authenticity. Some of these mass-produced, low quality product lines are not even made by people who believe in magick, or the art of crafting. These people only believe in making a buck at your expense.

----

1   *See list of recommended manufacturers and sources*

Sure, these products are very inexpensive and from a psychological viewpoint they may work in a placebo kind of way. I will admit that psychology can sometimes play a great role in the effectiveness of magick. To be sure, the best way to curse someone is to let them think that you have. Their own imaginations and paranoia will do the rest. Of course, I am in no way recommending that you curse anyone. I am just illustrating a point. To my way of thinking there is no substitute for authentic and quality products. In my opinion, a quality product is made using quality ingredients and is based on lore, intent and magickal synergy. The resulting product should be designed to work along the lines of solid magickal theory and philosophy and finally they should be made by people who believe in what they are doing. These are the criteria that I use to judge the quality of a magickal product, as these are the criteria by which I formulate my own products.

As I've already said, you will not find spells or recipes in this book. You will find examples of ways in which you can use the various magickal products that are available today. The lists of examples I give are not exhaustive, as I believe that no such list can be given. The ways and variations that the different magickal products can be used are as limitless as the imaginations of the users. You will see that I express this sentiment often in the book, as I believe it is a fact that bears repeating. I think that all too often people are lead to believe that there is one right and only true way to craft and that is simply not so. Hopefully, each and every crafter will find their own preferred ways to craft. Hopefully, each and every crafter will be guided by their own intuition and imagination, for these are the real tools of manifestation.

The Foundations of Formulation

Magickal Theory and Philosophy

Magickal products are built upon the foundations of Natural Magick[2]. The basic philosophy is that all things in nature are imbued with certain qualities or energies. This goes not only for those tangible things that we can touch, but also for sounds, colors, smells and so on. Along with these naturally occurring energies, there are those qualities that are culturally or historically acquired or pertinent. This is an over-simplification to be sure. There are lots of fancy terms I could use like "The Doctrine of Signatures" or "The Law of Synthesis" to name but a few, but what it really boils down to is that everything has an energy and that energy can be focused towards a specific goal or intent.

So, every plant, every rock, every mineral and metal, every liquid, every animal and each of its parts has a naturally occurring energy that makes it sympathetic towards certain goals, desires and needs. When we seek to use those energies to help us attain those goals, desires and needs, it is called using magick, it is called crafting.

___

2   *Also called Low Magick, Earth Magick and various other monikers.*

Intent-The Beginnings

Intent is always first and foremost. Regardless of whether we are talking about the formulator or the user of a magickal product, the beginnings and culmination of any magickal product, as well as any magickal working, is the intent.

For the formulator of the magickal product there are two basic areas of intent - magickal intent and intent of form. In other words, as a formulator, I must know what magickal intention the product will be designed to manifest and/or what form the product, or tool of manifestation will take.

It is the intent of the formulator that guides the creation of the magickal product. It's what guides and focuses the magickal energies of the ingredients and finally, it's the intent of the user that calls the magickal energy of the product to his or her purpose.

The Magickal Ingredients

When we need to formulate a product of magickal intent, we need only to look to the natural world for ingredients with the energetic qualities that we desire. Whether we look at those qualities from a chemical, physical or magickal point of view, these qualities do in fact exist. As modern day practitioners of the magickal arts, we benefit from literally thousands of years of research, lore and tradition. Humans have been observing, experimenting and recording this plethora of information concerning available energy for at least as long as we have been writing things down. Much of the work has already been done for us. We have but to access the information that is available to us, as well as our own innate intuitive sense to access this wealth of energy and magick.

The majority of the ingredients that I use in the formulation of my magickal products are botanical in nature and I suspect that the same would be true for most manufacturers of authentic magickal products. When I say botanical, I mean plant based or derived. That could be anything from dried elder berries to sweet almond oil, hyssop essential oil to apple cider vinegar, cocoa butter to rice.

That being said, there are many ingredients that are not plant based. There are the rocks and minerals such as sulfur and salt, gems and stones like quartz and rubies, animal products like lanolin and milk and the insect products like honey and bees wax.

Naturally, the ingredients are first dictated by the intent. Another consideration when deciding on the ingredients will depend on the final form of the product such as an incense, an oil blend or a candle. Yet another consideration will be synergy. For example, will this herb work well with this oil? The question of synergy may be energetic or it may be based on some other quality, such as scent. In most cases, these things can really be only learned by experience.

Non-magickal Ingredients

There are some ingredients in magickal products, especially when the products are to be sold to the public, that are often included to help the formulator achieve a stable and viable product that has a reasonable shelf life. Some people frown on the use of these products, because they are not natural. I would like to point out though, that no matter how manmade some of these products might seem, they are still derived at their core, from natural products.

Any formulator of quality magickal products will keep these ingredients to a minimum. That being said, the reality is that without them, the availability of many fine magickal products would become extremely limited and very expensive.

The Formulations

When a magickal product is being created, the formulator knows which is which ingredient is being added for its magickal energy and which ingredients are being added as catalysts, carriers, emulsifiers or preservatives. This knowledge is important. Knowing whether you are adding an ingredient for its magickal energy or for its ability to manifest the form of the product, guides the formulator in focusing the energy or not focusing the energy.

While each and every ingredient has its own energy, magickal quality or function, by combining them into synergetic formulas or products, we create better, more focused and efficient tools to help us manifest our needs and desires.

To illustrate, let's compare the making of a sword to the making of a magickal product. A sword made of iron is definitely a tool for fighting; it stabs, it slashes, it generally does the job of fighting and it definitely gives the sword wielder an advantage over the unarmed man. But when iron is alloyed with other elements or ingredients and certain processes are applied, the resulting steel sword makes a much better tool for stabbing, slashing and general mayhem. It becomes more than the sum of its parts, due to processes used to create the final product.

This is very similar to the making of magickal products. For instance, if I want to make a magickal charcoal incense, I could simply use one dried herb that I know has the qualities and energies that I require for the working. That would indeed be a tool of the working. I could, on the other hand, combine several herbs, resins and oils that correspond to my magickal goal, place them in a jar and allow them to mingle and blend their energies for a certain amount of time. To further enhance the quality of the incense, I might add certain ingredients in a specific order, to better facilitate even blending. To further enhance the magickal properties of the incense, I might add a certain gemstone to the incense jar or I might even mix it with a spoon made of a certain material or even expose the jar to the light of the sun. I might also mix it during a certain phase of the moon.

When I am done, I should have a magickal incense that is energetically appropriate for the desired magickal intention. The resulting incense will also be more than the sum of its parts, due to the process or processes that I use to achieve the final product.

Another aspect or reason for the blending of different ingredients, is that seldom is any magickal intention one-dimensional. No matter what the goal, there are always multiple aspects to that goal. These can be addressed by blending multiple ingredients, each chosen for its ability to address these multiple aspects or layers.

The formulator might also want to utilize different types of energies, such as elemental or planetary energies to the mix and again, the intent of the

14

formulator is playing a big role here. He or she knows that they are adding borage flowers to a prosperity herbal blend, so as to bring in the planetary aspects of Jupiter. In that way, the formulator is directing the planetary aspect of the ingredient towards the greater goal.

The Process

While I cannot assume to speak for all formulators of magickal products, I can share a bit of the process, at least my process, in formulating and making magickal products.

There is more than way to skin a cat, so to speak, and there is more than one way that a new magickal product is born. More often than not, a new product comes into being because someone has requested it. For instance, one of my shop customers asked me if I could formulate a Road Opener oil, as she had several requests from her customers for such a magickal oil, so began my quest.

So, I set about studying and thinking about the different aspects of that intent. I looked at it from many different points of view. What magickal, planetary and elemental energies would facilitate the real world elements that must be in place not only for manifesting the opening of new roads and opportunities, but also the ability to recognize and take advantage of them. Truth be told, this was one of the more complicated quests, as there are so many layers to the goal. (Some intents such as love or prosperity, while still being multi-dimensional, are easier if you are formulating a general love or prosperity product. If I was making an oil or other product for a specific person, I would of course have to take into account the many layers or aspects of that particular person's needs or goals.) Having broken down the magickal intent into several different layers of intent, I now had to decide which oils I would use for each of those layers. (Sometimes, one oil might fill the need of more than one aspect of the intent, but even so, that must be identified and considered when creating the formula.) I also had to think about whether or not I might want to add or utilize ingredients other than oils.

It took a few months (sometimes I am a bit slow), but eventually, I formulated a Road Opener oil that I was happy with and sent off a sample to my customer. She was so pleased that she asked for a complete line of Road Opener magickal products.

The basics and many aspects of the magickal intent were already worked out, but I still had to work on formulations for each type of product.

Each type of product has its own set of requirements and characteristics to be considered. The process of formulation, for any magickal product, is driven by form as well as intent. To formulate a magickal charcoal incense, I have to look at a larger list of possible ingredients, as my magickal incenses are combinations of herbs, resins, woods and oils. I also have to take into consideration how all of these possible ingredients smell when they burn and the order in which they should be added in order to achieve a thorough blending and how they will smell together. In formulating and designing a magickal candle, I have to take into consideration colors, layers of colors, oils, herbs and stones. Then, of course, there is the synergy of all the different ingredients to take into consideration.

Experience and intuition are also of the utmost importance during the formulation process. Experience and intuition tell us what works well with what and, in the case of an oil, that means both energetically and scent. Of course, the energy of the final product must be correct for the intent, but the scent should also convey the energy and depending on the probable use of the product, the scent may need to be one that can be worn on the body so it should be generally pleasing, or at the very least, tolerable. Another thing to consider would be whether or not a certain stone or root or metal might need to be infused into the oil as well.

Proportions, at least in the case of an oil, incense or other scent oriented product, are usually decided by strength of scent and strength of aspect towards the complete intent, by trial and error and finally, by patience. Formulating an herbal blend must take into consideration magickal association, strength of aspect towards the final intent and synergy, but it does not warrant the care in regards to final scent. So you see, each product has it's own set of circumstances and requirements.

Sometimes, such as in the case of traditional formulas, more than one version of the formula may already exist. In such cases, the formulator must do some research and must understand the intent of the formula. There are always variations in proportions and often there are optional ingredients as well. A really good formulator can improve on even the most time-tested formula. Of course, it has been common practice for the formulators of old to leave out an ingredient or two, or to misrepresent a proportion when writing down their recipes. It is in this way that many have sought to protect their own formulas.

So you see, both the intent and the type of product drive the process. Each type of product has it's own set of requirements and options and each intent has its own set of possible ingredients. All of these factors must be considered and decided upon by the formulator.

Intent-The Culmination

The last step in any crafting with a magickal product, the final touch to a successful magickal product, is the intent of the user. Whether you purchase the product or you make it yourself, or even if someone makes it for you, until you call the energy to your purpose, the work is not done. The formulator of the product has the responsibility to make the best product that they can and to make it with the proper focused energy and intent. It is your responsibility, as the crafter, to focus and aim that intent towards your goals and hopefully, to do so ethically.

Truth be told, the moment you decide to take the proactive steps of crafting, you begin to craft. With that decision, you put your intent out there, so to speak, and thus begins your crafting process.

Herbs & Herbal Blends

Herbs, and their derivatives, are the building blocks upon which all of my products are based. In fact, that is true of most authentic magickal products. The inherent energies of plants can be characterized and categorized in various ways. Magickal powers, gender, planetary energies, elemental associations, healing qualities and relationship to certain deities, to name a few. All of these energies exist and are available for us to work with[3].

Most metaphysical shops carry at least a few magickal herbs and some carry magickal herbal blends[4]. Herbs can be used alone, but my personal feeling is that a synergetic combination of herbs is much more effective magickally than just a single herb. But there are, of course, exceptions to almost every rule.

---

3   *I do not believe in "commanding" any natural/magickal energies to do my bidding. Rather, I believe in "working with" these natural energies.*
4   *The really cool ones carry my magickal herbal blends. (Oops, more shameless self-promotion).*

Magickal herbal blends are designed to work together, sometimes on many different levels or with the different types of energy all focused towards the magickal goal. These blends can be used in the creation of other magickal products, or they can be used alone.

Infusions

One of the easiest ways to use a magickal herbal blend is to infuse it in water or some other liquid. The resulting infusion is technically a potion and can be used in any way a potion can be used. (See Potions chapter for more info)

Oil Infusions

Infusing the herbs in an oil base creates a magickal oil. It may not be as fragrant as one blended with essential and fragrance oils, but it is magickally charged none-the-less. Once the oil is infused you can always add other oils for scent or to enhance the magickal properties of the oil. (See Magickal Oils chapter for more info)

Charm Bags

Charm bags almost always have at least one or two herbs included. The herbs are often allied with other items such as stones, charms, oils and any number of possiblities. (See Charm Bag chapter for more info)

Herbal Pillows & Packets

Stuffing a small natural cloth bag with a magickal herbal blend is a great way to carry your craftings into your dream state. A small pillow or packet can be placed inside your pillowcase or if you prefer a larger dream pillow can be made and placed on top of your normal sleeping pillow. Prophetic dream pillows are very popular. But, there are certainly other valid uses for the magickal dream pillow such as protection magick if you feel you are being assaulted in your dream state or a peace or sweet dreams pillow if you are having trouble letting go of the trials and tribulations of the day.

The same type of small natural cloth bags can be stuffed, sewn up and carried with you or placed in some appropriate place such as a protection packet in your car, a prosperity packet tucked into your purse, or even a

fertility packet between your mattress and box springs. A fishing success herbal blend could be sewn into your favorite fishing hat.

Herbal Poppets

A poppet is a doll that is used to symbolize a person who is the focus of a magickal working[5]. Poppets made out of cloth can be stuffed, partly or in full, with a magickal herb blend appropriate to the working. This could be a healing herbal blend to aid in healing either yourself or another. Perhaps a banishing herbal blend to loose weight or get rid of a nasty habit. Make a poppet of yourself and stuff with a prosperity herb blend to attract money into your life.

Floor Sweeps

Floor sweeps are herbal blends (or powders) that are scattered about on the floor. This is especially useful for cleansing, banishing and purification workings. The scattered herbs are swept up or even vacuumed up and disposed of. The theory being that the herbal blend absorbs the offending or unwanted energies and then you sweep them up and throw them away. This is a great way to cleanse a room after an illness, or to purify a temple space or even to get rid of those unwanted bits and pieces of tension still lying about after your in-laws finally go home.

Strewing Herbs

Once upon a time, no home was without herbs strewn about the floor. This was usually done to sweeten the air or to discourage vermin such as fleas and lice. (Yes, the good old days were smelly and itchy!) The same practice has many magickal applications. Prosperity herbs can be strewn about your place of business. Love herbs can be scattered about your bedroom floor. Protection herbs can be sprinkled around your home or even around the inside of your car[6]. Consecration herbs could be strewn about your altar or sprinkled over an item to be consecrated.

---

5   *It is considered by most to be unethical and manipulative to make and use a poppet symbolizing another person without that person's consent.*

6   *Take care about what kind of herbs you sprinkle around in your car. Very many magickal herbs look suspiciously like the very illegal "herb".*

Magickal Barriers and Enclosures

Herbal blends can be used to make a barrier of protection, or they can be used to surround a person or a thing with a certain energy. An enclosure of healing can be made by encircling an injured or sick person with healing herbs. A barrier of protection can be made by sprinkling protection herbs across the threshold.

Herbs & Candles

Herbs and herb blends can often be used in association with candle magick. A ring of herbs encircling a burning magickal candle can add more power to the spell. Once a candle is anointed with oil, a small amount of an herbal blend can then be rubbed onto the candle, or the herbs and oil can be mixed before hand and then rubbed onto the candle[7].

Charms and Talismans[8]

There are some very effective herbal talismans that are simply a sprig, a root, a twig or even a leaf. These can be carried, hung or even placed in your shoe. There is scads of lore concerning this type of use. One that pretty much everyone has heard of is the lucky four-leaf clover. I think that we've all spent some of our childhood sitting in a patch of clover eagerly searching for that special and powerful good luck charm. Here are a few other examples; carrying a High John the Conqueror root for success in court, carrying a nutmeg for prosperity or a cross of Rowan wood tied with red thread for protection.

Magickal Herbs in the Kitchen

I could and perhaps will someday, write a whole book on the various ways that we can use herbs to marry the art of crafting to the culinary arts. So many of the herbs that we use today for magickal work can and are used in the kitchen to transform the bland into the flavorful. With a little research, imagination, intent and conjuration, we can transform the bland into the magickal!

---

7   *Extra care should be taken when using dried herbs around candles as the herbs are likely to be quite flammable.*

8   *While not technically a magickal product, many of these herbs are available at metaphysical stores.*

One word of caution here, always use herbs that you <u>know</u> are safe for human consumption. Do not let the lure of magickal success or potency seduce you into using herbs that could cause yourself or others to have any adverse side effects. A good rule of thumb is to limit your ingredients to what can be found in a spice aisle at the grocery store. If you want to be a little more adventurous, you can always peruse the spice aisles of an ethnic grocery store too.

Really, it can't be said enough. The possibilities are indeed endless.

Magickal Oils

The term "Magickal Oils" really encompasses a great many things depending on your perspective. Like herbs, each oil has its own set of magickal and energetic properties that can be characterized and categorized in many different ways. Also like herbs, each individual oil can be used alone or in combination with other oils for magickal pursuits. My personal preference for magickal purposes is to use a synergetic blend of oils focused towards the magickal intent. There are many different types of oils that can and are used to create magickal oil blends.

Types of Oils

Essential Oils

Technically speaking, these are oils that are extracted from plant matter through a steam distillation process. These are pure, undiluted oils. There are other forms of distillation in use today and these other methods make it possible for us to have pure plant oils that were at one time unavailable, because the technology wasn't available. Oils extracted by these other methods are not known as essential oils in the oil business. Some are called absolutes, concretes, attars, CO_2 or SCO_2 extracts and so on. Each of these different names relates to the process by which the oil is extracted from the plant material. I usually refer to them all as pure essential oils or PEOs.

These oils are pure extracts from the plants, so they retain the magickal and energetic qualities of the plants from which they were derived, making them the perfect choice for magickal work[9].

Alcohol Extracted Oils

This is a method by which I make some of my most popular oils. The active properties of the plant material are extracted by infusing the plant material in some form of high proof grain alcohol, much the same way as many healing herbal extracts are made. Then the plant material is strained out and the alcohol extraction is gently heated with a prescribed amount of base oil. As the alcohol evaporates, the active constituents of the original plant material are transferred into the oil. Once all of the alcohol is gone, you have an extracted oil. Well, technically what you really have is a plant extract suspended in an oil base.

Infused Oils

Magickal oils can be made by infusing the plant or other material in a base oil. The idea being that the properties of the plant material are transferred into the base oil. The infusion is often helped along by gently applying heat. Infused oils are quite commonly made for healing home-remedy oils, but the same process and theory applies when making magickally infused oils.

This process makes a perfectly fine magickal oil, but they often have very little scent. Infused magickal oils are a great way to use herbal blends [10] to create magickal oils for various uses. It is also a great way to obtain a magickal oil that is unavailable. For example, mistletoe with all of its wonderful magickal properties, is simply not being distilled into a pure oil.

9   *Some books and some formulators will assign different magickal energies to an essential oil and the herb from which it is derived. I have never understood this and I personally don't agree with the philosophy.*
10   *See chapter on Herbs and Herbal blends.*

But, by infusing a base oil with fresh or dried mistletoe, one can infuse the oil with the energy of the plant. It is also a great process by which to infuse the oil with the magickal properties of other ingredients such as stones.

Synthetic or Fragrance Oils

Synthetic oils are popular with many formulators for many reasons. Even with the advent of the technology that allows manufacturers to produce some of the once unattainable oils, there are still some oils that are not widely available and some that are still not available at all. There are also some oils that are so expensive that they are unrealistic for most of us like jasmine or narcissus. There are also some oils, mostly from animal sources, that are politically incorrect to some degree or another or are downright illegal. These include oils like civet, musk and ambergris. So the world of synthetic and fragrance oils fills the void.

Oil Blends

Some formulators and some oil manufacturers have been able to almost perfectly mimic the scents of some of these unattainable oils by blending various pure essential oils together. Sometimes these recreations are created using a combination of PEOs and synthetic oils.

Carrier Oils

These are the base oils that are used to dilute and to help facilitate the blending of the magickal oils. Carrier oils are either completely unscented or very slightly scented, depending on the oil. Almost all good quality carrier oils are technically speaking, pure essential oils. The most common quality carrier oils are sweet almond oil and jojoba oil[11] but there are many other good oils used in formulations today. The choice of carrier oil is sometimes decided by magickal association such as using olive oil as a base for Abramelin oil and sometimes it is decided by the form that the finished product will take, such as using hemp seed oil for magickal bath oils because of its dispersing quality.

---

11   *Jojoba oil is actually a liquid wax.*

Formulation and The Great Oil Debate

There exists in the magickal community a great debate concerning the use of pure essential oils versus synthetic or fragrance oils and this debate basically boils down to two different magickal philosophies.

The first and most evident is that essential oil, being a pure extracted oil from the plant material, is the only way, other than infusion or extraction, to access the magickal properties and energies of the plant. A good solid magickal philosophy, to be sure.

Then there is the school of thought that suggests that it is the scent of the oil that creates the magick. This too is a solid theory. There are companies who have spent thousands upon thousands of dollars coming up with just the right scent to influence us, as consumers, to do certain things like stay in a casino longer or linger in certain areas of a department store longer or to evoke manufactured emotions on amusement park rides. Their money has not been wasted, it really works. The knowledge that certain scents evoke certain emotions, memories and attitudes is nothing new. This is simply another case of modern science proving what ancient crafters knew all along.

In my opinion, both philosophies are valid and the best way to formulate magickal oils is to work with both philosophies. Whenever possible, I use the essential, extracted and infused oils. When necessary, I use fragrance or synthetic oils. The final scent of the oil is a major part of the synergy and effectiveness of the oil as a magickal tool of manifestation. While I will always prefer the more natural oil, if a synthetic oil needs to be used to make the scent "feel" right, then so be it.

In some ways, formulating a really good quality magickal oil is one of the toughest formulations of all. All of the same magickal theory and philosophy are at play, but must be balanced with the final scent. This can sometimes be very tricky and often it may take months or even years to achieve success. There are a quite a few oil blends that I struggled with for some time before I was satisfied with the result. Once the formulation is perfected for the specific purpose, it is blended into a base or carrier oil. The reason for using a base oil is that many essential and fragrance oils are just too strong to be used on human skin without causing bad things

to happen, like contact dermatitis, so they need to be diluted. The base or carrier oil also facilitates the blending and melding of the other oils into a cohesive product.

Magickal oil blends are also often the main magickal ingredient in many of the bath & body magickal products. While some of the other ingredients may be chosen for their magickal qualities, the magickal oil blend used to scent the product is usually the main source of magickal energy.

Using Magickal Oils

Magickal Oil Blends are extremely popular for a variety of reasons. One of the reasons for this popularity is their ease of use. Magickal oils, can be worn just like perfume oil, they can be used to anoint a person or thing. They can be diluted and used in the bath and any number of other applications are possible. They are usually in small bottles or vials, so they can be easily and discretely carried around with you. Like any magickal product, the possibilities are limited only by the imagination of the user. That being said, let's look at some of the better-known uses.

Perfume Oil

Worn as a perfume oil, magickal oils work either on the wearer or those who come in close contact with the wearer, or a combination of both. To explain; if you are wearing protection oil, you are wearing it to protect you from outside forces that might attach, harm or otherwise attack you. If you are wearing a love oil, the theory is two-fold. On one hand you are the object of the energy. Theoretically, the energy of the oil will draw love to you and make you more open to opportunities to find the love you are looking for. On the other hand, those who come in close contact with you are going to enter into that sphere of energy and may in fact be drawn to you.

Sometimes a magickal person may choose a magickal oil blend as their personal scent and by that I mean beyond a specific working. For instance often a crafter will choose an oil that is blended to associate with a specific deity to attune to the energies of that deity. I wear Morrigan oil, because She is my matron goddess. A devotee of Isis may choose to wear an Isis oil blend. A crafter may also choose to wear an oil that they feel will work constantly to increase their magickal power or their wisdom. One might also choose to wear a planetary oil or an astrological oil to better attune to those energies.

Anointing/Consecration Oil

Another popular use of magickal oils is that of anointing. By anointing something we impart some energy to that thing. We might anoint an oak wand with a Horned God oil to consecrate it to the Horned God. We might anoint a magickal charm bag with an oil designed to further empower the magick of the bag. Often we anoint others or ourselves as they come into a magickal circle. The anointing serves as a consecration and as a denotation that we are transcending the mundane, that we are magickal beings entering into a magickal space.

Magickal Balms & Salves

I've included magickal balms and & salves under the heading Magickal Oil Blends, because they are really just magickal oils made more solid by adding wax, animal fat or a vegetable butter[12]. There is in truth, not much difference except for consistency and they can be used pretty much interchangeably when it comes to using them as a perfume or for anointing purposes. It's pretty much just a matter of personal preference.

Diffusing Oils

Magickal oils can be also be burned in an aromatherapy diffuser. This works in much the same way as magickal incense but without the smoke. The oil is placed in the heatproof bowl or vessel of the burner, along with some water. A small candle is then placed a certain distance from the bottom of the vessel. The heat from the candle gently heats the oil and water, which creates evaporation. The magickal oil is carried and dispersed with the water vapor. It's like a smaller, more subtle version of the vaporizer our moms used when we were kids.

Aromatherapy is so popular and mainstream these days that finding a burner is as easy as trotting down to your local department store. Of course, many metaphysical shops carry them as well and you may find a design that better suits your tastes.

12   *Witches Flying Ointment is another story all together and is addressed in a separate chapter.*

Magickal Incense

Incense is probably one of the most frequently used and best-known magickal product on the market today. The many functions it plays in modern crafting are only accentuated by the fact that it so immediately and directly affects our senses.

Incense can play a subtle supporting role in a working or it can be the major tool of manifestation. Simply burning the right incense can alter the energy and vibrations of a room or space. Incense can set the mood and mind-sets of the participants in all kinds workings like meditation, divination, spell-work or full-blown Sabbat rituals. It can be used to cleanse, purify and banish. It can be used to purify, consecrate or sanctify. It can focus, energize or soothe. The uses are literally vast and limited only by your imagination and desire.

Incense has historically been used for mundane as well as magickal purposes. In ancient times, it seems there was a plethora of unpleasant smells about, and burning fragrant herbs, resins and such helped to mask these odors. Magickally, incense was probably first used for mainly religious purposes such as temple consecration and purification, as well as being an acceptable and standard offering to deity. Eventually though, we figured out that the same philosophy that dictated the use of certain substances or combinations of substances to purify and sanctify the temple or holy place could be applied to almost anything, hence the development of magickal incenses outside the realms of the religious.

Truth be told, even today a substantial portion of magickal incenses are geared towards deity worship and various aspects of temple manifestation but the use of magickal incense to help in achieving the goals and aims of various other magickal workings is still a very valid and popular practice. In my own product line for example, blends such as Banishing, Cleansing & Protection and Prosperity are just as popular as the deity blends like Isis, Hecate, Goddess of the Moon and Horned God.

How Magickal Incense works

The same philosophy that applies to the energy and magickal properties of botanical ingredients such as herbs, resins and essential and fragrant oils, applies to the energy and magickal properties of incense.

Magickal incense works by way of the smoke. The different herbs and oils combine to form a synergetic blend with fire as the necessary catalyst. As the incense burns, the energies are released via the smoke and into the air and thereby affecting the energy of the room or space.

In some cases, the smoke from the incense is used to empower, cleanse or purify. In instances such as this, the smoke is directed by some method such as fanning or blowing it towards the intended object or in the case of smaller things, the object is actually moved through the smoke instead of moving the smoke towards the object. In either case, the smoke is what carries the energy. Using magickal incense is actually an excellent way to release and work with the energies of plants and oils.

Types or Forms of Magickal Incense

If you're like me, you'll end up using different forms of incense at different times, since each has their own advantages and disadvantages, such as necessary tools, time requirements, availability and costs. Here is a list of the most popular forms of magickal incense on the market.

Charcoal Incense

The most traditional form of magickal incense is charcoal incense. This type of incense is a mixture of botanical ingredients such as resins, fragrant woods and oils. This type of incense must be burned on a hot charcoal, hence the name charcoal incense. If circumstances permit, it can also be added to a smoldering fire with a good bed of coals. Conversely, yet much less efficiently, the incense can also be thrown into a raging fire, but it usually burns so quickly that little or no smoke is produced.

If, like me, you grew up a Catholic who had the honor of witnessing a traditional Mass, you may have seen a priest swinging a metal censer (incense burner) with lots of lovely fragrant smoke pouring out of it. This was most likely the result of a resin incense, since resins do produce a wonderful amount of smoke.

The use of charcoal incense is considered by many to be the traditional and preferred method of burning ritual incense and many crafters favor this method for all types of magickal work. I will say that when it comes to cleansing a house or banishing unwanted energies, charcoal incense is probably the most effective but it can be a bit trying when it comes to your smoke detector, as charcoal incense does produce a copious amount of smoke.

To use charcoal incense you will need a safe, fireproof (Fire-proof not heat-resistant) container to hold the hot charcoal and burn the incense. Any magickal shop or online store worth its salt will carry at least one or two varieties of charcoal incense burners. They are often called censers or braziers. These burners come in many forms but the most common and least expensive are usually made of brass and come from India. Often you can also find burners crafted out of soapstone, ceramic materials, glass and so on.

Depending on the design of the burner you may also need some sort of material to dissipate the heat from the charcoal, otherwise bad things can happen. If using a brass censer, the brass becomes very, very hot and then when you pick up the burner, you scream and disrupt the whole working. Another possibility is burning a hole or less than attractive scorch mark on whatever surface the burner was sitting on. Even more exciting is the unintended ritual fire, now that's always a crowd pleaser! Of course, the working will probably be a wash, but you'll have a good story to tell all your friends!

If you are using a soapstone, ceramic or glass burner without a dissipating material, the immediate result will probably be a broken or shattered burner which can lead to some of the same dramatic results as the brass burners.

The most common heat-dissipating material is sand. Today you can find all sorts of colored sands and sands from exotic places and, of course, the old stand-by, regular sand or colored sand, just like the stuff we had in our sand boxes as kids. In fact, it is the same sand we had in our sand boxes as kids. A couple of alternative options for dissipating the heat of the charcoal are to use table salt or even unscented, non-clumping and clean kitty litter. While these alternatives may not seem as glamorous as black Hawaiian Beach Sand, they are never the less just as effective. Whatever heat dissipating material you choose, you simply fill the burner about 2/3 full. You will have to use a bit of common sense here, as the depth of the burner will obviously dictate how full it should be. The charcoal should sit high enough to get sufficient oxygen and to allow the smoke to escape but not so high that pieces of hot charcoal may fall out of the burner giving you yet another chance at an exciting, but unintended ritual fire.

Having discussed how to dissipate and thereby protect not only your incense burner but also your surroundings and yourself, ethics dictate that I also tell you that as long as a dissipating material is used, you can burn charcoal incense in almost anything. A glass ashtray, a teacup, a dessert plate or whatever you have on hand, as long as it is not flammable, can be easily converted into a quick, makeshift censer with a little imagination and the right amount of dissipating material.

The other thing you will obviously need is charcoal. Charcoal incense is burned on special charcoals - no not the same charcoal briquettes you use to burn your steak on the grill! These special charcoals are usually in the shape of discs that has an accelerant (usually saltpeter) already added in. This special incense charcoal should also be available at any decent metaphysical store, but it can also be found at Catholic supply stores. An equally appropriate and well-suited charcoal is sold to hookah smokers and

can often be found at smoke shops and Middle Eastern grocery stores. In theory, the saltpeter accelerant should make lighting the charcoal very easy - in reality it is not always so. Charcoal has a shelf life in regards to the accelerant and that shelf life is greatly decreased from the moment you open the package. Keeping opened and non-opened packages alike in some type of airtight container can extend the shelf life of your incense charcoals.

The proper and safest way to light a charcoal is to use one of those long butane lighters - I call them fire-wands - that you can purchase at any grocery store somewhere close to the barbeque charcoal and lighter fluid. Place the charcoal in the burner, on top of the sand and hold the flame of the fire-wand next to the charcoal until you see tiny sparks moving their way across the charcoal. This is the proper and the safest way, but the most commonly used method is to hold the charcoal between your thumb and forefinger and hold the flame of a lighter or fire-wand next to the charcoal until you see tiny sparks that move across the disc, at which point you put the charcoal into the burner or on the sand, hopefully without burning yourself. Of course, I am not recommending that you light your charcoal this way, since that would be highly irresponsible of me, due to the fact that your chances of getting burned are greatly increased when using this method. I fully recommend that you light your charcoal the proper way. (A word of warning, if you should choose, against my recommendations, to light it the improper way...be very wary of doing so if you are wearing acrylic nails or nail polish. I have seen more than a few flaming fingernails just prior to ritual. It seems that acrylic nails and nail polish are quite flammable.)

Another good and safe option is to use a pair of metal tongs to hold the charcoal. Of course a good pair of kitchen tongs will do, but if you look around a bit you can find nice tongs at antique or second-hand stores. In times gone by it was quite normal for a well-prepared hostess to have a nice pair of ice tongs for preparing cocktails and these are often rather nice looking and you can sometimes find pretty silver or silver-plated tongs. You can also look at the smoke shops and Middle Eastern grocery stores because dedicated hookah smokers use tongs for their charcoal.

Once lit, the goal is for the charcoal to develop a fine layer of gray ash over at least part of, but preferably over the whole disc. By the way, in case you haven't figured it out already, let me point out that the lighting of the charcoal should be done at least 5 minutes prior to the time you are actually going to use it. If you try to put the incense on a charcoal that is not ready, chances are you will succeed only in putting out the charcoal.

Unless you burn through a lot of incense (pardon the pun), sooner or later you will come across the piece of charcoal that refuses to light. This may cause you to sigh, curse and consider the lighter fluid sitting by the grill…but don't do it! Once again, this is another recipe for ritual disaster. The best way to light a stubborn charcoal is to hold it with a pair of metal tongs over a gas flame like the one on your stove for example. It will take some time, since you are not really lighting it as much as you are trying to get it to the point where it starts to glow and ash over. Once you see that grey ash and the glowing red underneath, you know the coal is ready.

One final thing to consider when using charcoal incense, is what to do when the working is done and there's still this fairly sizable piece of glowing, red-hot charcoal to deal with. One option is to leave it in the burner until it goes out on its own. This is the easiest way to go, but should only be done if it can be done so safely. In other words, it's really not a good idea to leave a potential fire source unattended, especially if you have cats! Another option is to smother the charcoal with sand, dirt or salt. This is a very effective way to put it out, but once again, err on the side of caution and make sure it is really out before doing anything else with it, like throwing it in the garbage! One more option is to douse the charcoal with water. However, I really don't recommend this method because it can create lots of stinky smoke, it makes a mess of the burner, and if you are using special sand or other heat dissipating material, you will probably turn that into a very interesting form of mud.

Self-Lighting Incense

This form of incense is a relative newcomer in the world of spell crafting. Self-Lighting incense is usually a powdered wood base that is often colored and scented with oils. It also contains a fair amount of saltpeter, which acts as the accelerant, thus eliminating the need for charcoal. Since it is inexpensive to produce, it is usually inexpensive to buy and it often comes in very vibrant colors that make it quite attractive to some practitioners.

Honestly I have never been a fan of this type of incense as it always seemed a little too artificial for me, but there are many who are very fond of it, so by all means try it out and form your own opinion. You will still need a fireproof dish or burner of some kind to use this type of incense but you will not have to deal with the charcoal[13].

Stick & Cone Incense

The use of stick incense is actually very old. In Asian countries such as Japan, China, and Tibet, incense makers have been preparing, hand rolling, and hand pressing incense into sticks, blocks, logs and cones for centuries, using powdered herbs, woods and fragrant oils. These traditional types of stick and cone incense are still made today in pretty much the same way, with the exception that now machines often do much of the work that was originally done by hand. While this type of incense is lovely and usually of fine quality it usually only comes in single scents like Jasmine or Sandalwood. However, this in no way means that these sticks cannot be used for craftings. While the traditional sticks were not formed on a stick, but rather the material was formed into a stick, it is from this type of incense that our modern day stick was derived.

Today, stick and cone incense are the most well known types of incense and are often burned for their scenting qualities rather than their magickal qualities. Stick and cone incense is available almost anywhere from gas stations to department stores. Modern day stick and cone incense is usually made by dipping or soaking unscented sticks and/or cones into a mixture of scent and cut oils. The resulting incense is then dried and packaged. Some incense makers, such as myself, add another step. When the sticks are almost all the way dry, I coat them with powdered herbs and/or resins. It's really a nice effect and really adds to the overall quality of the incense.

There are those among us that shudder at the thought of using this type of incense for magickal or ritual work, as they feel it is non-traditional. In my not so humble opinion, they need to get over themselves. While my personal preference for most ritual and magickal work is indeed charcoal

13   *If you do have self-lighting incense that doesn't want to light, it's probably because the accelerant has somehow been compromised by moisture perhaps, but whatever the reason, if this happens you will probably have to resort to burning it on a charcoal after all.*

incense, there are times and places when stick or cone incense can be just the right thing. Let's face it, burning charcoal incense takes not only a certain amount of time and preparation, it also takes some specific tools and accoutrements. Stick incense in particular can be more than accommodating to the modern day crafter on the go. It can usually be both lit and put out quickly, can be disposed of easily once the hot tip is put out, and it is very easy to improvise an incense burner if you don't have one. I have seen soda cans and bowls of dirt for example serve as adequate stick burners. Cone incense on the other hand requires a more fireproof vessel. It does not get quite as hot as incense charcoal, but it can still produce a good bit of heat so care should be taken. Again, a dish of sand, salt or even dirt will do in a pinch.

Another advantage is that if there are people around you who wouldn't find the idea of magickal workings appropriate, stick and cone is incense is so commonplace today that probably no one would even give it a second thought.

It is true that many manufacturers of stick and cone incense use the cheapest oils and other ingredients possible like some of that stinky, artificial smelling stuff you sometimes see in gas stations and from some street vendors. On the other hand, there are also manufacturers, like myself, that make really high-quality incense with high-quality ingredients and intent.

One of the great things about sticks and cones is that, due to the minimal equipment needed and the fact that it is so non-threatening to most people, simply lighting and burning this type of incense can be a small working all on its own. No one else need be the wiser; the only other tool needed is your intent as the crafter.

Smudge Sticks

This form of incense is also a relative newcomer, but in actuality it's been around for a very long time. What is fairly new is its use by non-Native Americans. Smudge sticks are bundles of herbs, usually, but not always, some form of sage, that are tied with cotton string and then dried. To use a smudge stick, the end is lit and then the user either blows on the

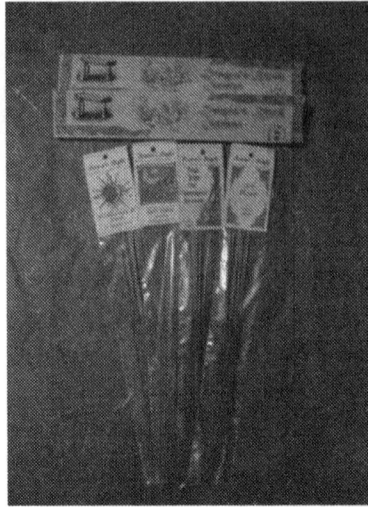

smoldering herb bundle to keep it smoldering or fans it with feathers. Native Americans have been using this type of incense for centuries. The most common uses of smudge sticks are in the areas of cleansing, purification, and banishing, but where there are magickal people, there are imaginations at work, so I am sure that smudge sticks are being used for all sorts of intentions these days.

This is a very pure form of incense as there is no accelerant used. Applying fire and directed oxygen to the sticks produces the smoke, and then the user directs the smoke as needed or desired. In fact, this is such a pure method, that many purists think only Native Americans should use it and only for its prescribed and traditional reasons. In addition, some purists feel that sage, most specifically white sage (salvia apiana) is so sacred that it should never even be sold. The problem is that white sage and smudging are so popular now and there are so many companies built around this type of product line, no one's going to be able to get that cat back in the bag.

I do have to admit that smudging is very effective for certain things but it does have some drawbacks, besides those related to the ethics of non-Native Americans using it. For one thing, quite a few people are actually allergic to the smoke of white sage to some degree or another. While I don't have any real proof other than personal observation, I would estimate that 10-20% of people have some degree of adverse reactions to the smoke. Of course, it doesn't help matters any that when people use smudge sticks they tend to waft it directly into your face. (So, for all of you out there who like to go around unbidden, smudging everyone at public events, stop it!)

Some of the adverse reactions that I have seen are itchy eyes, headaches, and throats closing up, although I am sure there are others. It is my suspicion that some people don't even realize that it is the sage that is giving them the headache and not the 'heavy energy' of the ritual. When I had my store, we facilitated a lot of public and semi-public rituals and it became a policy to discourage using white sage, due to the many people that I knew personally who were allergic. It does put a damper on a ritual or other magickal working when you have to stop everything because one of the participants has suddenly quit breathing. In all fairness though, white sage is not the only botanical that is used to make the traditional type of smudge sticks. Other herbs, such as but not limited to desert sage, yerba santa and mugwort are also traditional Native American smudging herbs and these do not seem to cause the same reactions as the white sage.

Another drawback to using smudge sticks is that it is very high maintenance since the stick only produces the desired smoke while someone is fanning them or blowing on them. However, in some cases this can be advantageous. Since the bundle will only smoke while someone is tending to it, it goes out very quickly, eliminating some of the fire hazards discussed earlier with other methods. If you want to use this type of incense though, the maintenance issue can be avoided by simply using the dried herbs like any other charcoal incense instead of using the smudge bundles. There are lots of lovely loose smudging blends on the market today and they are also very easy to formulate yourself if you are so inclined. These are burned in the same way as traditional charcoal incense.

How to Use the Different Varieties of Incense

There are lots of standard incense blends and scents available in the various types of incense. Some of them are pretty straight forward like burning love incense for a love spell or banishing incense to banish bad luck but there are also lots of blends that have multiple uses. *(These examples are by no means exhaustive lists of the many and varied uses of any incense blend. Rather, they are listed simply as examples so that the reader can better understand how to use the different blends available today)

Deity Incense

Deity blends that carry the name of a specific deity are presumably blended in honor of and in association with that specific deity. These blends are naturally good choices if you are seeking to honor, worship, or call upon a certain deity but the uses do not stop there. Often these blends are quite appropriate for certain seasonal rituals and workings, as well as magickal workings that would benefit either from the help of the deity, or if the general personality of that deity relates to the working.

For instance:

Brigit incense would be appropriate for Imbolg and all type of Spring rituals, as well as transformative workings (due to Brigit's smith association) or healing rituals (due to Her healing associations) and workings for new starts or new beginnings.

Hecate incense would be appropriate for Dark Moon workings and anytime you wanted to strengthen the magickal or sorcerous power of a spell.

Horned God incense would be appropriate for any type of male energetic empowerment and all types of fertility and passion.

Aphrodite or Venus incense would be appropriate for any love, lust, or peace workings.

Elemental Incense

Elemental incense can be used to attune to the spirit and power of the elements in ritual and in crafting.

Water incense would be appropriate for certain types of healing workings as well as compassion, meditation, and wisdom and knowledge spells.

Earth incense would be a wonderful incense for any prosperity or manifestation workings.

Fire incense is great for ambition, transformation, and lust craftings.

Air incense would be appropriate for intellectual workings, travel, and change.

Seasonal or Sabbat Incense

This type of incense, while being originally blended to honor and celebrate the seasons and/or Sabbats, also has many other uses. The seasons and the Sabbats have underlying mysteries and burning this type of incense anytime it is appropriate - not just during the specific season - can access those energies. In fact over the years I came to rename most of my Sabbat incenses, due to the fact that the demand was still present, even long after or long before the season of the Sabbat.

Beltane/Sacred Marriage is a great incense for working of perfect unity, balanced love and fertility.

Cornucopia/Lughnassadh incense is appropriate for any working of increase or thanksgiving.

Solar Joy/Summer Solstice is great for any success, getting the better job, victory or higher goal workings.

Winter Solstice would be appropriate for craftings to do with rebirth and hope.

Ancestral Spirit/Samhain incense is great for divination workings, working with the ancestors *(tapping the bone) or workings to cross the veil. *(Travel to the other lands, the lands of the dead or the ancestors)

Planetary Incense

Planetary incense also carries with it all of the associations attributed to planets such as:

Venus incense for love and passion.

Mars incense for courage or victory in battle.

Saturn incense for overcoming oppression or conversely, for bindings.

Single Scent Incense

Single scent and/or single ingredient incenses, also have multiple uses and a little knowledge or research and intuition will reveal a plethora of uses for each one. You need only look to any book with a good list of associations to find many uses for single scent incense. *(What I am referring to is incense that bears the name of a single scent such as Jasmine or Patchouli, but often these single scent incense also include other ingredients that are usually added to compliment the scent.)

Frankincense can be used for almost anything like consecration, success, healing, power, banishing and so on.

Rose for love, compassion or peace.

Patchouli for lust, manifestation or banishing.

Sandalwood for meditation, healing, purification.

The Choice is Yours

So whatever your needs or desires, when it comes to magickal incense you have a great many options. When preparing for or designing a specific ritual, crafting, spell or working, you can see that your options for appropriate incense are vast and varied and ultimately the choice will be yours to make.

Don't be afraid to experiment not only with the various forms, but also with the various scents. So, for a love spell, you might choose a love charcoal incense blend or perhaps a Venus planetary stick or perhaps an Aphrodite self-lighting powder or maybe just a stick of rose incense. If you wanted to burn a good incense before meditation, you might choose sandalwood powder, a lunar charcoal blend or a meditation incense cone. If you wanted to banish the negative energies in a sick room after an illness you might choose a white sage and mugwort smudge stick, or burn some frankincense resin on a charcoal, or you could just light a healing blend stick incense. Experiment, explore and enjoy.

I would also like to suggest that incense is one to those little ways that we can bring a little magick into our everyday lives. For example, why not burn a little house blessing incense a couple of times a week or little love incense in the bedroom from time to time. The magickal and the mundane are only as far apart as we make them.

Potions

From the Dictionary:
po ·tion [**poh**-sh*uh*n] —noun
a drink or draft, esp. one having or reputed to have medicinal, poisonous, or magical powers: a love potion; a sleeping potion.

[Origin: 1300–50; ME *pocion* < L *pôtiôn-* (s. of *pôtiô*) a drinking, equiv. to *pôt(us)*, var. of *pôtâtus,* ptp. of *pôtâre* to drink + *-iôn- -ION*; r. ME *pocioun* < AF < L, as above]

—Synonyms elixir, brew, concoction, philter.
Dictionary.com Unabridged (v 1.1)
Based on the Random House Unabridged Dictionary, © *Random House, Inc. 2006.*

Many people, especially non-Magickal people, believe that potions are these nefarious liquids that must be drunk or somehow consumed to work their magick. While there is certainly a whole class of potions that can be consumed, the world of potions is much larger than just consumable liquids. For our purposes, potions are basically any magickal liquid concoction that is sprayed, sprinkled, poured or consumed. Oils are not usually classified or called potions, but it's really a matter of preference, so sometimes they are. These various and sundry liquid concoctions usually consist of a liquid or blend of liquids infused with one or more ingredients - that's the basics.

Potions are very effective due to the fact that the infusion process allows many ingredients to be combined into one synergetic product to do the deed, whatever that deed might be. There are many brands of potions on the market, but in my opinion, there are very few that are worth purchasing. The majority of potions available today are no more than colored water scented with some cheap synthetic scent with a label pasted on. No real intent, except for making profit.

Potion Basics

We already know that potions are basically a liquid infused with the inherent properties of one or more ingredients. The types of ingredients that can be used to make potions are unlimited, and the most commonly used ingredients are herbs or botanical substances. However, there are many, many other possibilities such as: gemstones, animal hair or parts, sea shells, bird feathers, insects, soil from specific places, metals, buttons, pins, all sorts of everyday items, even words* - and the list goes on.

The most common liquids used to make potions are water, vinegar, alcohol, and even urine, as well as other human bodily fluids, but it is possible to use other liquid and semi-liquids like milk, or honey.

Magickal words, symbols, charms and incantations can be written on paper and added to a potion.

To many of us today there are many old traditional ingredients for making potions that we find distasteful, disgusting, or against our beliefs. I do not condone or condemn their use I simply include them here for informational purposes.

Things to remember when making and using potions

Length of viability

When making your own potions, keep in mind that potions can spoil, most especially potions made with water and any other natural ingredient that can spoil on its own, such as herbs. A spoiled potion is not only unsafe to use, but the intent and magick of the potion can degrade and pervert, just as the ingredients do. If making a water-based potion, make only what you can use in a few days and keep it in the refrigerator when you are not using it. As a producer of commercially available potions that are water based, I have to add certain other ingredients to preserve the viability, such as cosmetic alcohol or some other preservative. Vinegar and alcohol based potions have a much longer shelf life. Even so, to formulators such as myself that intend on selling their wares, additives are necessary to extend shelf life and inhibit bacterial growth, no matter what the base liquid is. Nobody wants mold growing in their love potion, now do they?

Labeling

I am notoriously bad about not labeling potions, both made and in progress. More than once someone, usually a guest because my family knows better, has consumed or almost consumed, some horrible tasting potion left brewing in a cabinet or sitting on a shelf that I haven't properly labeled. So, for the sake of all those around you, label your potions. Another good reason to label is that you just might forget what something is, and nothing gripes my fanny more than having to pour a perfectly good, but unremembered concoction down the drain.

Examples and Guidelines for Using Magickal Potions:

Bath & Body:

Potions can be used very effectively in the bath water; in fact the bath water could be considered one very large potion! Just add an adequate or preferred amount of your potion under the running water of the bath. I suggest adding the potion to the running water because it helps to more thoroughly mix the potion with the water. It can, however, be added at anytime.

Other personal care type uses include using a magickal potion as a final rinse for your hair and/or body.

Examples:

- A meditation potion could be poured into a bath as part of a premeditation ritual.
- When washing a child's hair, a general protection potion could be poured over the child's hair as a final rinse.

Sprinkling or Asperging:

While most of us are familiar with the asperging of a circle or ritual space, the same philosophy can be used anywhere or for anything. An object, for instance could be sprinkled with a potion to imbue it with some quality or another.

Examples:

- A prosperity potion could be sprinkled on your wallet or around your place of business or even around your garage just prior to the annual garage sale. *Experience would dictate you will probably have to do that the night before, since there's always some wahoos that show up early!
- Sprinkle a healing or cleansing potion around a sick room.
- Sprinkle a passion potion on your sheets or a love potion around dining room prior to a romantic dinner.
- Sprinkling a potion of protection, such as Four Thieves Vinegar[14], across your threshold or even around the boundaries your property or even your car can be very effective.

Spraying, Misting or Spritzing:

Sometimes sprinkling just won't do, and let's face it, the spray bottle is part of our modern lifestyle. If the ancients had spray bottles, they would have used them. Spray bottles distribute a fine, or not so fine, mist on an item or around an area.

Examples:

---

14   *I even sell a "Four Thieves Vinegar To Go" that is a 2 oz. plastic spray bottle of Four Thieves Vinegar that can be tucked in a pocket, purse or office drawer and can be used whenever the need for a little protection is arises.*

- Keep a spray bottle of a protective potion or a peace potion in your desk drawer at the office[15].
- Spay a fine mist of focus potion around your computer or work area prior to or during study or writing.

Mop and Cleaning Water:
While adding potions to mop water is an extremely effective use, it is sadly not one of the most popular ones. I don't know if that says something about the general cleanliness of magickal people or if people just don't think of it.

Examples:
One of the most effective cleansing concoctions that I have ever seen is made by mixing Florida Water and blue balls[16] into a bucket, tub or basin of water and using the water as final rinse when cleaning any object, place or thing…even your body, if diluted properly. There is also tons of lore concerning herbal infusions that were used over the centuries for cleansing altars, and that same philosophy can carry over to include any magickal or mundane person, place or thing.

Consumable Potions:
Now here's a category of potions that I highly recommend you concoct yourself or have made by someone you know that you can trust. Anything, magickal or not, that you consume should be made under safe and hygienic conditions and should be made with only safe and nontoxic ingredients. Of course, I realize that there are many different philosophies as to what is safe and nontoxic, but I think you get my drift.

---

15   *I mention the office drawer because over the years I have heard time and time again about the negative energy that can prevail in any workplaces.*

16   *Blue balls are nothing more than balls of bluing. For those who are too young to know what bluing is, it is a substance that was much in use in days gone by as a whitener for laundry, as well as other applications. If you've ever seen a blue-haired old lady, it's because the hair rinse she is using to keep the yellow out of her grey had bluing in it and she's used too much!*

Alcohol and water are the usual base liquids for consumable potions, but other liquids can be utilized as well. While palatability is certainly something I would suggest when considering a base for a drinkable potion, it is certainly not a required characteristic. The only real requirement is consumability. In other words, is it safe to drink?

A word of warning concerning *Gem Stone Elixirs*; there are some very popular books out there that tout the healing and magickal qualities of gem stone elixirs, which basically consist of a liquid that has had some gem stone or another soaking or infusing in it. Now, I certainly have no problem with infusing a potion, oil or elixir with a gemstone, I do it all the time, the problem arises when these elixirs are actually consumed. The process and philosophy is definitely sound, but the resulting elixirs can be very dangerous to consume as many of our wonderful gemstones have constituents that can be toxic to humans such as arsenic, cyanide, or lead, to name just a few. So, if you are of mind to create a consumable potion or elixir that utilizes the qualities of the many gemstones available to us today, then do your research and be very sure that the stones that you are using are, in fact, safe to use.

There will of course always be those that want to push the boundaries of safety with little or no knowledge about what they are working with to achieve some dark and arcane potion for other world travel or flying or some such thing. Probably nothing I say will deter such folks, but I'll say it anyway….don't play with toxic botanicals. It leaves a yucky taste in your mouth and you just might find that your other world journey is more permanent than you intended.

Some Common and Traditional Potions

Four Thieves Vinegar

The legend of Four Thieves Vinegar is an interesting one. It seems that during one of the outbreaks of the Black Death/Bubonic Plaque, that there was a rash of robberies committed against the victims of this horrible disease. Now, this was doubly troubling to the authorities, due to the fact that not only were they getting away with the robberies, but because they were also doing so without getting sick. The implication being that they either had some kind of preventative or cure that was unknown to the medical authorities, or perhaps some magickal device of protection against the ghastly disease, which, I am sure, had some of the religious authorities somewhat perplexed and concerned.

Well, eventually the thieves were apprehended, and obviously there were four, hence the name of the potion. Anyway, they were given a choice by the authorities - either reveal how they were able to elude the disease and receive immunity for their crimes, or go the gallows. As you can imagine, the choice was a rather easy one to make. What they revealed was that a witch or gypsy had given them a recipe that they were to drink and to pour all over themselves before they were to go commit the robberies. Legend has it that they turned over the recipe and went on their way, never to be seen again.

Today, there are various versions of the recipe floating around and who's to know which the original was. In truth, it doesn't really matter. The main ingredients, are herbs that are all known today for their various healing qualities. These include, among other things, antibacterial, antibiotic and even pest repelling qualities. From a magickal standpoint, these herbs are also known as protective, hex breaking, and healing. The herbs are infused into vinegar and although the process is not difficult, it can be quite smelly depending on how you achieve the infusion.

Over the years, I have perfected my own version and there are many other good versions out there. However, one version I would recommend against, is the blue liquid that is sold as Four Thieves Vinegar but that I doubt very seriously has anything at all to do with the actual herbs or process, and is, as far as I can tell, just a smelly blue liquid. Anyone that is familiar at all with the herbs or with vinegar will able to take a whiff and know right away that it is not a true Four Thieves Vinegar.

Uses for Four Thieves Vinegar

The magickal uses of this potion are basically related to various forms of protection and healing. Once you know the legend, it is pretty easy to figure out the magickal properties of Four Thieves Vinegar. I would say that, under no circumstances, should you consume Four Thieves Vinegar unless you or someone you know and trust has made it, and that you can be sure none of the herbs used have any toxicity problems, like wormwood,

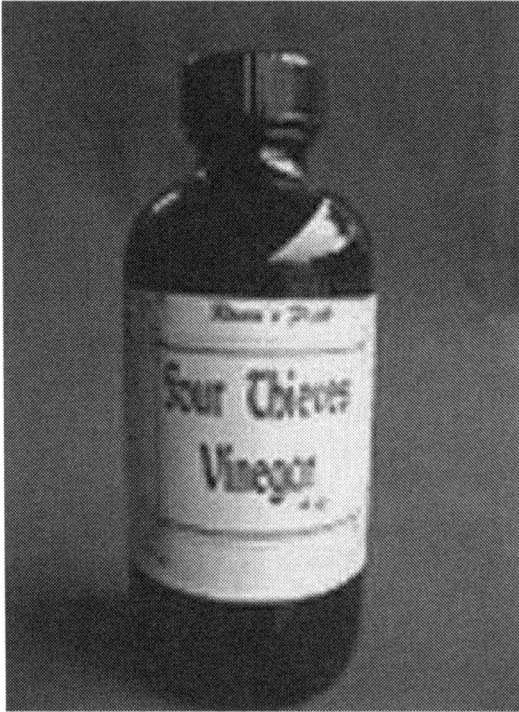

for example. Wormwood is one of the standard ingredients in any Four Thieves recipe and even though it has been used for centuries as a healing herb, it is one of those herbs that cause some nasty toxicity problems, like massive vomiting; it is a purgative, you know.

Truth is, if you would like to make a healing vinegar that can be consumed, then you need to be reading different books - books that more thoroughly explore the pros and cons of the various healing herbs, and books that explain the process and precautions necessary for creating healing herbal vinegars.

Florida Water

Florida water is a wonderfully clean-smelling toilet water to be exact. I am not exactly sure how it became part of the modern crafter's tool chest, but I suspect it came by way of Cuba and Santeria. If you've ever been to Southern Florida and you've ever been around one of those dashing, older Cuban men, you have smelled Florida Water. To be sure, it has been here in the States for a long time and it was once quite the thing for a man to use as an after shave, but I believe its magickal use came through Santeria. Not that it matters in the end - it does work beautifully and I do know that its use is much more common within the Afro-centric magickal communities, but like most everything else in our modern world, it has crossed over. And why not - if it works, use it!

The most popular brand of Florida Water is fine, but knowing what I know from making it myself, it is not what it once was. Never the less, it works. A true Florida Water is basically a citrus-based cologne diluted with various distillate waters, known in modern nomenclature as hydrosols, and known in days gone by as floral waters. It is mainly used for cleansing and purification and it is wonderful for those purposes. In my opinion, every crafter should have a bottle on hand, and besides, it smells really nice.

War Water

Now here's an interesting, balls out, old school potion! War water, if you hadn't already figured it out by the name, is a war potion that can be used in a couple of different ways. First off, it can be used to basically prepare for war, to ensure success. The other reason to use War water is to incite war. Basically, War Water is Mars Water.

Now is as good a time as any to discuss the differences between the real life, traditional meaning of war and the symbolic, metaphoric meaning that is often implied by modern magickal people. I assume I don't need to explain the traditional meaning, but the modern metaphoric meaning can be applied to almost any circumstances. That's as clear as mud! Let me try to explain; suppose you had to go to court to fight an ex-spouse for custody of your children. That could be a type of war. It is a battle, a situation that causes you to fight to win, such as a custody battle. Another example might be if you were a gardener here where I live, and the gophers kept eating your plants. The actions that you will have to take to try and remedy the situation, whether you choose to try and persuade or just annihilate, could be considered a war. *If you think I'm kidding, I'm not. I've seen men and women with determined fury in their eyes when it comes to gopher wars!*

The one and only required ingredient in War Water is rust. That's right, plain old everyday rust, usually obtained from an old style, non-galvanized nail. Why? Because iron was for centuries the metal of war, and even though we have many more options today, it is still imbedded deep in our cultural memory that iron is the metal of the God of War, and therefore the metal of war. This association comes from way back in the Iron Age, when the boys with the iron weapons were the boys that won the wars.

There are not so many versions of War Water on the market today, because it is so easy to make yourself, although it can occasionally be hard to come by a non-galvanized nail. It was years before I actually produced it for the public - of course, mine is not just rusty water. If you're inclined to make your own War Water, start, of course, with water and an appropriate nail, but if you want to infuse your potion with more power, try infusing the potion with one or more of the herbs associated Mars as well.

Water of Notre Dame

(aka Water of Peace)

In complete opposition to War Water, we have Water of Notre Dame. This potion was very popular at one time, but today, very few practitioners even know it much less use it. This potion is a combination of floral waters (or hydrosols as they are called today in the aromatherapy world) and oils known to promote peace and compassion.

I don't know much about the history of Water of Notre Dame, or how it came into being, but I do know that it is a wonderful potion that deserves a revival in these times of strife and anxiety. I hope that more people take it up as addition to their magickal cabinets; I think we could all use a little more peace and compassion.

Ultimately, I believe that you will discover that the many uses for potions are as limitless as your imagination. The more you use them, the more uses will find for them.

The Magickal Candle

Candle magick is an extremely popular form of magickal crafting and with good reason. It's quite effective. Once upon a time, a crafter's options in regards to candle availability were extremely limited, but no more. Due to modern technology and the evolution of wax and wax additives, we almost have too many choices today.

Candles have a long history of being used to provide illumination in the mundane sense of the word, so it is not surprising that they also have a long history of being used to provide illumination in the spiritual sense of the word. The use of candles as votive offerings goes back at least to the ancient Egyptians and perhaps beyond. Candles have long been a mainstay in religious ceremonies of all kinds and therefore, the evolution of candles to the more magickal uses only makes sense.

The flame of a burning candle can be mesmerizing, calming and meditative. Who hasn't been transfixed, even if only for a little while, by a dancing candle flame? These very qualities make candles a wonderful tool for focusing intent and calling the magickal energy to our purpose.

How Magickal Candles Work

Like magickal incense, the catalyst of the magickal candle is fire. Depending on the intent of the working, slightly different magickal theories are utilized. If the magickal intent is one of drawing something to you like love or money, then the fire releases the intent, sends it out to the universe. If the working is a petition, then it sends the petition to the deity being petitioned. On the other hand, if the purpose of the working is to take something away, like a banishing, then the fire burns up that which is being banished. It is the intent that directs that action of the candle.

There are actually many types of magickal associations or philosophies that can be employed in candle magick. Color, shape and ingredients can all play a part in the empowerment of the magickal candle. Other forms of crafting are often applied as well. One magickal candle may be empowered by herbs, oils, stones, sigils and color or any combination of these. Also, due to the fact that wax actually holds a shape when cool, whole other areas of magickal symbolism can be utilized.

Magickal candles can be made, or candles can be made magickal. I realize that this statement may seem a bit redundant or confusing. To clarify, a candle can be made from the very start as a magickal candle or alternately any candle can be made into a magickal candle.

Making a Magickal Candle

Making a magickal candle involves much the same type of process as any other magickal product. Like all other magickal products, the vehicle or medium carries with it a certain set of requirements that must be considered. The formulator, or in this case we might say the candle-maker, starts with the intent and design and then makes the candle with colors and ingredients chosen to synergistically work together to accomplish the magickal goal. Candles can also take various forms and each form requires certain processes, such as certain types of wax and sometimes other additives to create a quality finished product. All of these things must be taken into consideration by the magickal candle-maker.

Magickally made candles are usually found as votives or pillar candles. There are some really finely crafted magickal candles being produced by

ethical crafters that can be found online and at your local magickal shops. These are usually in the form of votive or pillar candles, but there are sometimes other types as well. For instance, I make magickal jar candles. The jar allows me to address the different aspects of a magickal goal in different layers. Each layer may be a different color and have different ingredients in it.

Formulated, or made magickal candles, can be a bit pricey in comparison to regular candles, but rightly so in my opinion. Much time and effort goes into making any type of quality candle. Making a magickal candle requires more effort and time, at least when it is done properly.

Making a Candle Magickal

All of the various candles available to us today are potential magickal candles, regardless of whether they are bought at a metaphysical store or your local department store. The simplest unscented white taper candle can be empowered to even the most complicated magickal goal. That being so, imagine the possibilities that are available to you when you consider all of the different shapes and colors and even scents that are readily available.

There are two things that are absolutely necessary to make an everyday candle a magickal one. You need a candle to empower and your own focused intent. Everything else that you do adds to the crafting. The same philosophy that applies to the other magickal products applies to candles as well. When we use multiple ingredients and processes to create a product, like a magickal candle, we create a tool of manifestation that it greater than the sum of its parts.

The process of applying oils, herbs, sigils or what have you to the candle, is often called "dressing" the candle. Common sense and intuition can be great guides for dressing a candle or you can consult the many books available on magickal correspondences and/or candle magick.

The more common types of candles are available most anywhere. Tapers, votives and pillar candles can be purchased at your local metaphysical shop or just about anywhere else. Metaphysical shops may also carry jar candles. These are clear glass jars with the candle poured into them. Alternately, but less commonly available, are pullout candles. In this case, the jar and the candle are sold separately. The reason for this is that the candle can be dressed and inserted back into the glass jar for burning.

Metaphysical stores or online shops often have a selection of candles made in traditional magickal shapes. These are various shaped and colored candles that have traditional or customary uses. Many are very easy to figure out and some are not. The variety and selection carried by the shop is usually guided by the primary focus of the particular shop.

Many specialty candle shops and department stores also carry candles in various shapes and colors that can be easily directed toward magickal use. One of the more obvious options is a heart shaped candle for a love spell, but there are many more possibilities, such as using a candle in the shape of a rabbit for a fertility spell[17].

One can sometimes find pre-dressed candles for sale. All that's needed is for the practitioner to call the energy of the candle to his or her purpose. There are also a few shops that will dress the candle for you, sort of a made to order candle-dressing service. Either pre-dressed or dressed to order, you as the practitioner, will still need to add your own energy and intent to the process, but that is the same with any magickal product.

Finally it must be said that, in truth, a candle can be made magickal even without dressing it. Focused empowerment by the practitioner can be all that is necessary to turn a dinner taper into a tool of manifestation. The dressing of a candle towards a magickal goal just employs more layers of magickal crafting.

The Wax

No discussion of magickal candles would be complete, in my opinion, without some mention of the different types of wax used to make candles. Today, the majority of magickal candles, indeed all candles, are made with paraffin wax. There was time when most candles were made from various solidified fats, such as beef fat, which is alternately known as tallow. Over the years, various other fats such as whale oil were used. Then,

17   *When buying what are often referred to as novelty or seasonal candles try to ascertain whether the candle was actually made to be burned or just displayed. Often a sticker or tag will give you that information.*

sometime in the 19th century, the process of distilling paraffin wax from crude petroleum was discovered and there was no turning back. Paraffin wax produces a much cheaper and better quality candle than the animal fat candles. No matter how objectionable some people feel about a wax derived from petroleum, it is still the least expensive and most versatile option available to us, even today.

There are various types of more natural waxes used in the manufacture of candles such as beeswax, bayberry wax and the vegetable waxes such as soy and palm wax. There is no doubt that these are wonderful waxes and more and more manufacturers are offering different varieties of candles made with them. Even so, they are still not quite as versatile as paraffin wax. Like it or not, the majority of candles that are on the market are still made from good old paraffin wax.

I do have to admit that there is something wonderful about a 100% pure beeswax candle. I often use them for adorations, but seldom for magickal work. I also make and sell bayberry candles around Yule time. This is another favorite of mine but again, this wax has its limitations. It is a very hard wax and has to be combined with paraffin and beeswax to make it viable as a votive candle. It's also a very expensive wax and as a result, my bayberry candles are pretty expensive. Having said that, I do always sell out.

Candle Burning Do's & Don'ts & Precautions

The catalyst that powers the magick of the magickal candle is fire and working with fire requires a certain amount of caution and common sense. As we all know, fire has many good qualities, but unguarded and unrestrained it can quickly become devastating.

A commonly used candle for crafting is the jar candle, also known as the 7-Day candle. So called because they are supposed to be able to burn for the equivalent of 7 full days[18]. There are people and books out there that will tell you to light a 7-Day candle and leave to burn for 7 days uninterrupted. Okay, so how is that a good idea? Unless you, or someone else, is going

18   *My experience has always been that these candles burn at different rates depending on magickal empowerment and intention.*

to be in attendance and awake for all of those 7 days, do not try this at home. In other words, do not leave a burning candle unattended. Don't be fooled into thinking that 7-day jar candles are safe to leave unwatched. They can get very hot, sometimes they crack or even shatter. Over the years I have heard all kinds of ways to safe-guard against starting a fire with an unattended 7-day candle and some of them sound pretty good, but the only sure way to safe-guard against a candle starting a fire is to not to leave a burning candle, of any kind, unattended for any reason. I cannot even count how many practitioners I know that have caused some degree of fire damage to their homes or the homes of others due to unattended candles.

Here's a trick I learned from a very smart witch years ago. When you have to leave or go to sleep, simply focus your attention on the candle flame, then close your eyes and visualize it burning on the astral plane, then put out the candle. Case closed, the candle is still working, only now it is working on the other planes and how can that be a bad thing? The candle spell is still working and you won't burn down your house.

Another issue with using candles is the melting and melted wax. While drip-less candles do exist, they are seldom employed as magickal candles, probably due to their scarcity and expense. This is really a three-fold issue. First, there is the problem of the melting wax. If the melting wax is hot enough, it can actually ignite a fire if it comes in contact with something flammable. While this doesn't happen very often, the possibility does exist. Even if the melting wax doesn't start a fire, it can make an awful mess, which is the second issue. So to solve both of these issues, some method for catching the wax should be considered. While there are a few good solutions for removing wax, the best defense here is definitely a good offense. There are a few candleholders that have catch reservoirs for melting wax, but for the most part we are pretty much left to our own devices.

The best option that I have been able to come up with over the years is to have some sort of a plate or bowl that can be placed under the candleholder. Use a little melted wax to stick the candle to the plate if you don't have a holder that the candle will fit in.

The third issue is what to do with the leftover melted wax. There are plenty of great books out there today that have lots of wonderful candle magick spells in them, but seldom do they ever tell you what to do with the leftover wax. What I suggest is following the spirit of intent for the working in deciding what to with it. If you were doing a spell to get rid of a bad habit, then take the leftover wax and bury it or put it into a paper bag and throw it away or throw it into a raging fire, the idea being to get rid of it. On the other hand, if you were doing a working to bring love into your life, I would suggest keeping the leftover wax. You could keep it someplace safe or pertinent to the working, or you could melt it down and make another candle with it. In other words, let the intent of the original working guide you.

Candles that are in glass jars, like the 7-Day, 50-Hour and pull out candles, obviously don't require a holder since they are in glass jars, but these jars do get very hot and can get hot enough to occasionally shatter the glass. Because of this, you should be very careful about where you sit these candles when they are burning. The extreme heat, while it may not shatter the glass, can scorch or burn a nice altar cloth or wood finish. In extreme instances they could even start a fire. This can also be true of glass votive candleholders. So please, take proper precautions with these as well. One more thing, the heat can travel all the way up the jar, so please don't grab a burning or recently burning jar candle with your bare hands, it hurts.

Bath & Body Products

Technically speaking, many of the products discussed else where in this book could also fall under this category. I am using this classification for all the other items that didn't fall under one of the previous categories. Conversely, many of the products addressed here could have been included in other categories, but since I'm writing the book, I get to make the categorical inclusions. Unless of course, the editor put his foot down.

There are oodles of bath & body products being made today for magickal purposes. Many of them are so self-explanatory that there's not that much to say about them, but I will attempt it anyway.

Bath Salts

As the name implies, the base medium of this product is salt or a mixture of various salts blended with oils, herbs or colorants. Occasionally, the mixture is even charged with stones or other items.

Salt has a lot of wonderful qualities that are very successfully applied to magickal work such as cleansing, purification and banishing. Some of these qualities may not seem advantageous to certain magickal intents, such as prosperity or love. The trick is to view the salt as an agent to cleanse and clear away the obstacles to your intent so that the oils and other ingredients can work more effectively towards that goal.

Not only does salt have the ability to absorb oils and color without losing its basic structure, but it also holds a magickal charge very well, making it a wonderful vehicle for carrying the magickal energy and intent. Many of you may also be familiar with the practice of sprinkling salt & water around the temple space during, or prior to ritual circle construction. There are a couple of different philosophies that support this practice and that help to explain the effectiveness of bath salts. One philosophy is the same as we've mentioned before and that is that salt is purifying and cleansing.

Another reason or philosophy for using salt and water in the circle construction is Elemental. Salt is representative of the Element of Earth and Earth is the Element of manifestation, so it goes to figure that by adding salt to your spellcrafting bath, you are helping to manifest your intention[19].

Another common practice is to use salt as a protective barrier against unwanted energies and/or entities[20]. Therefore, using salt in the magickal bath provides a protective barrier between you and any unwanted and unseen forces that are lurking about. This could be seen as especially important when working to draw something in. Better to keep out anything else lurking about[21].

---

19   *In this type of circle construction, all four Elements are represented, for example; salt for Earth, water for Water, candle flame for Fire, and incense smoke for Air.*

20   *This practice may very well have evolved from the practice of preserving food with salt. When food, especially meat, is prepared with a salt barrier, it prevents spoilage.*

21   *The logic of this statement will depend greatly on your own point of view when it comes to unseen entities or forces. There is a school of thought that suggests that when we work magick, we create an energy that can be visible and attractive to 'magickal' creatures.*

Salt Scrubs

Salt Scrubs are usually used by those who prefer showers to baths. They are basically very similar to bath salts, except that the salt and other ingredients are blended into an oil base. The same magickal principles apply, but there is one major difference. Due to the high oil content of scrubs, you will probably notice a stronger residual scent. Due to this fact, salt scrubs are actually gaining in popularity, especially when it comes to magickal intentions such as love, prosperity or luck.

If you would like to experiment with salt scrubs, but can't find products geared towards your goal, you can try mixing magickal bath salts with a good base oil, such as olive oil or sweet almond oil. However, I would suggest only mixing what you can use immediately, unless you have the necessary additives to adequately preserve the blend. Also, I suggest never using salt scrubs on your face or any other delicate areas, as most salt is just too abrasive. Another word of warning, be very careful getting out of the tub or shower after using oil based scrubs, because you're likely to be kind of slippery.

Soap

Magickal soaps are pretty self-explanatory. Soap is the base medium for oils and/or other ingredients geared towards your specific goal or intention. This is definitely one of those times when intent really guides the use of a magickal product.

Magickal soaps can be the tool of the crafting in and of itself, such as a cleansing, banishing or purification with the soap actually be the tool of the crafting. It is actually the soap that is cleansing, banishing or purifying you. This is fairly straightforward and logical, since soap by its very nature is for cleansing. Sometimes however, magickal soaps are used as yet another level of reinforcement to the crafting. For instance, any of the many intentions of attraction, such as success or love, could be reinforced. Using magickal soap for such an intention may seem illogical in comparison to an intention such as banishing, but it is simply a matter of a different approach and philosophy. For intentions such as love or prosperity, the magickal soap cleanses away obstacles to the desired goal. On another level, the magickal ingredients that have been included and blended into the soap also leave a magickal residue that stays with you, almost as if you were wearing a magickal oil.

There are absolutely tons of great magickal soaps on the market today and many great soaps being made at home, largely due to the invention of melt and pour soap bases. These bases make it very easy to create all kinds of marvelous soaps. The soap base is simply melted and then oils and other additives are blended in and then the soap is poured into molds. Melt and pour soaps are usually glycerin based. Due to the growing numbers of vegan consumers, most bases are completely animal product free, but if this is something that is really, really important to you, you might want to check the label very closely.

The more traditional type of soap is created by blending what basically boils down to fat and lye. Ironically, in the soap business this process is known as cold-processed soap. What makes it ironic is that when these two ingredients are combined, they actually create a great amount of heat. The process that creates the heat, and ultimately the soap, is a chemical process known as saponification, in other words "makes soap". This method of soap making is a lot more time consuming and requires quite a bit more in the way of time, know-how and tools, so it is far less common to find magickal soaps made in this way.

Bubble Bath & Body Wash & Shampoo

Magically speaking, liquid soaps and body washes work in the same way that solid soap does; same philosophy of use, same procedures, just a slightly different form. It really comes down to personal preference and availability.

Shampoos too, are very similar except ,of course, that the main area of concentration is the hair. This is not really a very popular type of magickal product. Due to the fact that the area of concentration is limited, the magickal uses seem a bit limited as well.

Bubble baths, which are really just liquid soaps with extra foaming agents, do seem to have their own special niche though. There is a psychological aspect to a luxurious bubble bath that can really add something to certain types of workings. I will admit that the energy of a bubble bath is a bit subtler than that of magickal bath salts and soaps, but sometimes it's just the ticket. It must be, I sell tons of them.

Body Mists and Sprays

Body mists and sprays work with the same philosophy that magickal oils do, but with a bit of a lighter touch. Basically, they are sprayable potions made by blending oils into a base that is either alcohol or water based with added ingredients to emulsify the oils into the base and often a preservative as well. The basic idea is that the alcohol and/or water quickly evaporate, leaving behind the magickal oils to do their work. It's actually quite great.

One of the things I really like about magickal body sprays and mists is that they can be applied more liberally, more often and over a greater area. These mists and sprays can also be sprayed on an object, such as a piece of paper, a talisman or what have you.

Magickal Lotions and Creams

There was a time in the not so distant past, when any lotion or cream that claimed that it could make a woman appear younger was considered to be magickal. Today, there are lotions and creams that are formulated for all sorts of things including beauty and youth, but that also run the gamut from power to healing. Again, it is the same philosophy that applies to magickal oils being applied to the body, although the affect is a bit subtler. Of course, there is also the added benefit of being moisturizing as well.

Magickal Body Powders

There are magickal powders and then there are magickal body powders. In a sense, they are quite similar but then again, there are some pretty strong differences too. Magickal body powders tend to be very fragrant, they are usually a pretty color and they are often quite sparkly. Like many magickal body products, these are often geared towards intentions like love, lust or passion, but the possibilities are endless. Protection, success and prosperity powders could also be quite effective, to name just a few of the possible applications.

Body powders are made by blending a powder base such as talc (ooh,

yucky, stay away from these if at all possible)[22] or more natural powdered bases, such as cornstarch or arrowroot powder with oils, powdered herbs and various other ingredients to add color, sparkles and to ensure flow.

Besides working along the same lines as magickal oils and herbs, magickal powders can also be used as barriers against negative energy or illness. Magickal powders can be added to shoes to encourage speed, or swiftness. Sparkly powders designed to aid in the attraction of love or passion can be powdered all over. Healing powders could be rubbed into the hands of someone just prior to using the hands in a healing working.

Magickal Bath Oils

This type of magickal product works in much the same way that magickal oils do, except with magickal bath oils, we are adding water into the mix. A truly better description would be that we are using water as a method of distribution, as a vehicle so to speak.

Bath oils are made by blending magickal oils into a specific kind of base oil. To clarify, I should say if it is a good magickal bath oil, it is blended into a base oil that disperses evenly along the surface of the water. Many of the common base oils used in making magickal products are great for a great many things, but not great for bath oil. The less than ideal oils will pool up in one area on the surface of the water, rather like an oil spill. While a non-dispersing bath oil is not nearly as disastrous as an oil tanker spilling crude out on the ocean, it is still not a good thing. To work effectively a bath oil needs to be present on the whole surface of the water, that's not to say that a non-dispersing oil wouldn't have some degree of effectiveness, but I have always felt that a quality magickal product should be a quality product and getting a whole lot of oil concentrating around your knees is just not as good as having the oil equally and completely dispersed in the bath water. You see, one of the ideas behind bath oils in general, as well as magickal bath oils, is that when you get out of the tub a thin film of the oil will remain on your body and you wouldn't want to be caught like Siegfried

---

22   *Talc or talcum powder is known to have fairly high quantities of arsenic. I prefer to avoid it all costs.*

[23] or Achilles[24] with one part or another being left vulnerable or with out the magickal energy directed towards your goal now would you?

While I personally love a good bath oil, I feel that they do have one major drawback and that is the oily residue left in the tub. There are a couple of reasons that is really unwise to leave that residue unattended to. If someone else gets in the tub before you have cleaned it out, you will subject him or her to the magickal residue left in the oily residue that's left in the tub. Another good reason is that whoever next steps into that tub, and it could be you, will have the opportunity to experience one of those all to frequent accidents in the home. In other words, someone could slip and fall and break something. So, if you do use a bath oil, magickal or otherwise, you should really clean out the tub when you are done.

While I have tried to cover all of the magickal bath & body products, I am sure that I have left out a few. The thing to remember is that the possibilities are endless. Any product that can be made - can be made magickal. All it takes is a little imagination and ingenuity. If you want a take a magickal bubble bath but can't find a product that suits your needs, then improvise. You could make an herbal infusion that can be poured into the bath water along with some regular bubble bath. If you want a magickal shampoo, but can't find one already made, then add a few drops of magickal oil to your shampoo.

---

23   *Siegfried, a character in Wagner's epic opera Der Ring des Nibelungen, lost his life due to the fact that his assailant was able to stab him in the back, the one area of his body not magickally warded.*

24   *The classic Greek hero Achilles was made invulnerable to attack by his mother. When he was an infant, she held him by one heel and dipped him into the River Styx. The problem being, that while he was invulnerable everywhere the water touched him, the water did not touch the heel by which his mother held him. He was later slain by a wound to that unprotected heel.*

Odds & Ends

These are various magickal products that didn't really fit into any of the other categories, at least by my estimation, so I've included them here.

Magickal Inks

The basic philosophy of magickal ink is that by using it, you are magickally empowering the words that you write or the symbols and sigils that you draw with the magickal energies of the ink.

Basically, a good writing ink must be liquid enough to use yet thick enough so that an adequate amount sticks to the writing instrument. Equally important is the pigment used to color the ink. It must be dark enough and long-lasting enough to be legible for a great many years.

Whether a good magickal ink must have all the qualities of a good writing ink is a matter open to debate. One could argue that for most spell crafting purposes, the ink need not be legible for many years as it is the writing or drawing with the ink that imparts the empowerment to the crafting.

Besides, often times the paper that the magickal words or sigils are written on is burned or in some other way destroyed.

On the other hand, I know of practitioners who write extensively with quill and magickal ink. Besides, not all magickal words or symbols are destroyed. Some are in fact kept for quite a long time.

So, to be on the safe side, a good quality magickal ink that is produced for sale to the public should be a good quality writing/drawing ink that is made with magickally chosen and focused ingredients. This is not as easy as one might think. There are lots of magickal ink recipes floating around, both ancient and modern. If you've actually ever tried making one, you know that what reads as a pretty simple process is in actuality not as easy as it seems.

Most magickal inks on the market today are in fact, just colored inks. Not many people are willing to take the time and energy to actually formulate an ink from magickally chosen ingredients. If you are lucky, you might get an ink that is at least scented with a magickal oil or that has at least some powdered herb or something added to the ink to empower it. From a magickal standpoint, these can work. From a traditional standpoint, these are but cheap and easy imposters. The choice is as always up to the magickal consumer. Truly magickal inks will be more expensive, but I think they are well worth it.

There are all sorts of magickal inks for all sorts of magickal purposes, but there are three magickal inks that are the most well-known and most commonly used inks for crafting purposes. All three are red inks.

Dragon's Blood Ink- A general all-purpose magickal ink and the most popular of all.

Bat's Blood Ink- Made from a Dragon's Blood base with other botanical essences. This ink is sometimes used for more manipulative types of craftings such as hexing, crossing or binding but it is also used for banishings.

Dove's Blood Ink- Also made from a Dragon's Blood base, this ink is typically used for all sorts of love spells and petitions.

Magickal Powders

Sadly, many of the magickal powders on the market today, fall short of what I consider to be quality magickal products. They suffer from the same inadequacies that many of the potions, oils and incenses do. They are often no more than colored and cheaply scented talc. A good quality magickal powder may start with a powder base like maybe talc (1) or preferably something more natural, like cornstarch or arrowroot powder. Powdered herbs are added and often oils, all chosen to works towards the intended goal. Alternately, the powder base can be left out so that the ingredients consist of mainly powdered herbs that may or may not be scented with oils. As with many magickal products, color is yet another level of energy that can be applied towards the goal, so magickal powders are often colored with various possible additives.

Magickal powders are often used as floor sweeps, which means that they are sprinkled on the ground and swept or even vacuumed up. They may also be designed to be left on the floor or perhaps to be sprinkled across the threshold. For example, a protection powder might be sprinkled across a threshold to prevent negative or evil energies or even people from crossing said threshold. A banishing powder might be sprinkled on the floor and then swept up, the idea being that the powder absorbs that which needs to be banished and then is swept up and thrown out. A prosperity powder might be sprinkled on the floor of your place of business and then left there for the duration.

Magickal powders do in fact have applications that do not involve the floor. Sprinkle a passion powder on the sheets, a prosperity powder in your wallet, a study powder on the pages of a textbook, meditation powder on a candle used for meditation, protection powder in your car, a divination powder on your hands prior to handling your tarot cards. The possibilities are endless.

There are actually magickal powders that are designed to be blown into some one's face. In general, I am personally against this use for magickal powders. Besides the fact that it is very rude, it often borders on being unethical and it can be unsafe.

Room Sprays

In the Weird and Wacky Products section of this book, you will see that I mention Aerosol Room Sprays, but there are room sprays and then there are room sprays. The room sprays that I would recommend are very similar to the Magickal Body Sprays and Mists in use and formulation. The difference being that magickal room sprays are designed to spray rooms (or other areas) instead of people, like you couldn't figure that out on your own. In fact, most magickal body sprays and mists can be used to magickally spray or mist rooms, but I wouldn't go the other way around unless you are sure about the ingredients of the room sprays. Room sprays are sometimes formulated with much harsher ingredients, or at stronger concentrations, than body products and spraying the wrong thing on the wrong body part can be unfortunate, to say the least.

Potpourri and Sachets

Potpourri is a very popular fragrance and decorating accoutrement these days. Traditionally, potpourri was made to sweeten the air at a time in our history when the air really needed sweetening. The same process can produce a very nice magickal product that can be used for a myriad of possible applications.

Magickal potpourris should be made with intent and scent in mind so they can be a bit of a challenge to the formulator, but certainly it is a challenge that is worth rising to. They can be beautiful to look at, wonderful to smell and energetically powerful all at the same time.

The basic process for making potpourri is that various botanical substances are mixed with oils and placed in a sealed container to "ripen". The botanical substances are chosen for scent, color, aesthetic appeal or they may be included because of their fixative or preservative abilities.

When ready, the resulting potpourri can be placed around a room in pretty bowls or some other appropriate vessel and left to scent the room. Some types of traditional potpourris are designed to have their scent released by steaming.

To make a magickal potpourri, all of the same considerations apply with the added application of magickal properties. It's really not as difficult as it might sound, but it does take some thought and since quality potpourris require a ripening period of 6 weeks or more, it does take some time. The magickal versions are not widely available due to these factors. Truth be told, traditional quality potpourris made for magickal purposes or not, are fairly costly due to the time and ingredients that go into to making a really fine product. If you do find a magickal potpourri that is inexpensive, I doubt that it is traditional or very outstanding.

Since potpourris are designed to scent rooms, the magickal applications tend towards charging the atmosphere, as opposed to magickally charging a person or an item. Possible applications would include healing, general blessings, peace, meditation, harmony, passion and the list goes on and on. One thing to remember is that although potpourris require a ripening period, they have a fairly long shelf life as long as they are kept in air-tight containers.

Sachets are paper or cloth packets or bags that are filled with magickal potpourri or something similar. They are also often decorated in various ways and can be quite attractive. These packets are then put into your drawers with your clothes, or they can be hung in the closet with your clothing. The philosophy being that the magickal energy infuses the clothing as the scent infuses the clothing. (2)

Spell Kits

Spell kits can be very simple or very elaborate. The great advantage of spell kits is that the manufacturer has assembled all or most of the needed magickal products for you. This is great for those who don't have the time or the know how needed to gather all of the components for a magickal working. There are a couple of things that do bear mentioning though. For one thing, be sure to read the instructions before leaving the establishment where you are purchasing the spell kit. There are usually certain items that you will need that are not included in the kit. For instance an incense burner or a candleholder. Reading the instructions could save you another trip to your local metaphysical shop. If you are buying your kit online, ask if you will need anything else to complete the spell before purchasing the kit. Any ethical online shop should be more than willing to answer your questions. If they aren't, shop elsewhere.

The other thing to keep in mind, is that even with the best-designed spell kits, there may be room for improvisation on your part. For instance, if there is a chant or incantation that doesn't feel right to you, remember that the world as you know it will not come to an end if you change it. Rewriting the chant may be just the thing to make the spell more personable, more you.

Everything Else

While I have tried to cover all the bases, I am sure that I've forgotten something. If I haven't listed a magickal product, it is in no way an implied condemnation of the product. It just means that I either don't know about it or I simply forgot it.

(1) Today we know that talc has a high concentration of arsenic.
(2) The sachets described here are traditional ones. There are some magickal sachets that are being mass-produced that are no more than little bags filled with artificially colored and scented powders of some kind.

Weird & Wacky Magickal Products

Over the years I have come across some really interesting magickal products, admittedly, most of these are made by companies that I wouldn't buy stuff from, but they do bear mentioning. If, for nothing else but a slight comedic interlude.

Bath & Floor Washes

If you've ever had the dubious pleasure of experiencing a bottle of magickal bath & floor wash, you probably had the same initial reaction that I did, "What the heck is this stuff?".

Generally, they look thick and creamy and they come in lovely pastel colors like lavender, mint green and pink. Rather reminiscent of the old-fashioned diarrhea medicine we all grew up with. Some of them probably come in darker colors too like black or dark purple. I have opened and smelled one or two and the scent is really indescribable. To say they smell artificial would be an understatement.

The next thought that crossed my mind was how do you use it? I assume from the name that you can either pour it in your bath water or use it to mop your floor. Now, if we were speaking about an herbal infusion, I could totally understand the dual use, but I don't think I would ever pour that concoction into a tub of water that I was going to add my naked body too. Way too scary for me.

Want a product that you can bath yourself in and add to your mop water? Try an herbal infusion instead.

Aerosol Room Sprays

For those of you who haven't seen them, they look just like a regular can of aerosol room spray or air freshener, but their stated purposes are for magickal intents, not getting rid of the stench from junior's gym shoes. They're more geared for getting rid of Junior. Now, I don't have a problem with the basic premise or philosophy, it's the ingredients that I find unsettling and mysterious. Since there are usually no ingredients listed, I guess maybe the mystery is supposed to add to the magick. I much prefer a misting spray with known ingredients, not a bunch of really cheap chemicals. Remember, if you spraying it in a room, you're breathing it!

Animal Parts

Okay, so some animal parts are weird and some aren't. That's probably very hypocritical of me, but there it is.

There are the odds and ends that we come by naturally. Sometimes we find feathers laying about, we might use a chicken bone leftover from dinner or a if we are really lucky we might find a cat whisker. If you're hunter or a farmer, you would naturally have access to certain other animal parts. These are normal found or leftover items that we might incorporate into our spell crafting, but there are distributors that claim to sell things like swallow's hearts, black cat bones or wolf eyes. I have a couple of problems with these items being for sale. One is that chances are, what they are selling is not what they are claiming it is. There are manufacturers (and I do mean manufacturers) that sell totally bogus animal parts such as these.

Think about it, do you really think that there is someone breeding swallows or catching them for that matter, just so that they can cut out and dry their little hearts, not bloody likely! Likewise, for wolf eyes and black cat bones. As often as not, the black cat bones that they are selling are really chicken bones, doctored up and manipulated so that these less than reputable companies can manipulate you out of your money.

Of course, then there is the issue of ethics. If all of these products were in fact real and not manufactured, then somewhere, someone is dispatching black cats, blinding wolves, and slicing open swallows and bats by the hundreds simply so that we can have a supply of spell crafting items. If this were true, which it's not, but if it were, that would be so wrong. If someone really wants a bat heart for a spell crafting, then they should have to get it themselves! Better yet, find an alternative.

Another thing to remember is that there are many herbs that have common names that sound like animal parts. For instance, deer's tongue, cowslip, dragon's blood, toad and weasel snout, just to name a few. So when trying to replicate old spells, we really have no way of knowing, at least some of the time, if they are really calling for the tongue of a deer or simply the herb known as deer's tongue.

Graveyard Dirt

Okay, why sell or buy graveyard dirt? Is there really anywhere on this great green earth where there are no graveyards? I guaran-damn-tee ya, that 95% of all graveyard dirt sold in America today is just dirt. So, why buy it? If that's what you're going to get anyway, why not just use your own dirt? Mind you, I am not saying that there are no valid reason for using graveyard dirt, just that if you're buying it, you're probably just buying really expensive potting soil.

Another thing to consider is that just like certain animal parts, there are herbs that have been called 'graveyard dirt' at some time or another, in some place or another. Mullein, for instance has been known by that name. I guess the best advice I can give when it comes to using graveyard dirt, is that if nothing else will do, go find a graveyard and collect it yourself.

Mercury Filled Nutmeg

I know of only a few places where these dangerous little talismans can be purchased and I'm not all together sure that it should even be legal to do so. These are made by drilling a hole into a nutmeg, filling it with mercury and then sealing it with wax. Then these are to be carried around as a magickal charm. Mercury poisoning......need I say more?

Of course there's always the matter of authenticity to consider. It could very well be that no real mercury is used at all, which brings up another issue, namely authenticity. So, when people buy these talismans, they are either buying a lie or they are buying a talismanic time-bomb. Either way the consumer loses, in my opinion.

But wait there's more!

This is by no means an exhaustive list of the weird magickal products that are available today. It's just all the ones I can think of right now. I wrote this chapter as much to illustrate a point as anything else. Common sense is your best guide when it comes to purchasing and using magickal products of all kinds-common sense and intuition.

Witches' Flying Ointment

The magickal products discussed in this book are concoctions of herbs and other ingredients blended together to manifest various needs, desires and goals. Witches' Flying Ointment is indeed a concoction of herbs and other ingredients to manifest the goal of "flying" to the Witches' Sabbat. The real fly in this ointment, so to speak[25], is that this magickal product could kill you.

There is a dangerous attraction to these infamous concoctions that can take the casual dabbler to the very brink of death….. and sometimes beyond. Is it the associative taboo or is it some need or desire to escape the reality of our world that drives the curious to experiment with the dangerously toxic ingredients that are purportedly part of the recipe?

For centuries there has been much speculation and study as to actual recipe or recipes for Witches' Flying ointment. Oddly enough, though much has been written, no actual recipe has ever been found. At least not a recipe that can be connected with one of the unfortunates who confessed to

---

25   *Okay, I know it was corny, but I couldn't help it!*

using them. If the confessions of these accused diabolical women are to be believed, they learned to make the salves from the Devil and I guess he didn't allow anyone to take notes. Of course, it didn't help matters much that those who claimed to use the ointments to 'fly' to the Sabbat, were illiterate and therefore they couldn't write it down anyway. Any recipe that did exist was passed on orally.

What we do know, is that there were many ingredients that were confessed to being used and the ingredients were not always the same. What they did have in common was that they all included one or more plants that were and are known to cause altered states of consciousness. They were also known to be deadly poisons.

I have no doubt that there were people who made and used ointments with these dangerous botanical and sometimes animal substances and that these ointments gave them the feeling of flying, of visiting another reality. As reality for the peasant was not a very pleasant one in the Dark Ages, I can certainly understand why they would yearn for a change of scenery, even if it was only for a short time. The reality of the illiterate peasant during these times was a hard one and death was ever close, so perhaps they had little fear of leaving behind the misery of their lives.

The statistics on drug use and addiction in our modern culture show that even though times have changed greatly since those Dark Ages, the desire of some of us to escape reality has not. So, it makes one wonder if the interest is truly magickal, or if it is really the hallucinogenic hayride that appeals to many of the curious.

Over the years, I have had many requests from customers for these dangerous herbs such as henbane, aconite, datura, hemlock and bella dona. I do not and will not sell these herbs. Besides the fact that there may be some legal implications, for me the ethical implications of selling people such toxic substances are far more important. Interestingly enough, if they really wanted them, if they had really done any kind of research, they would have been able to find these plants, but those with little knowledge always look in the wrong places.

92

I am certainly not condemning the use of certain botanicals by certain cultures as prescribed by their religious and spiritual traditions, nor am I recommending them. I myself have studied these botanicals and I have tons of books on ethnobotany. I have grown some of the herbs and collected some of them in the wild, but I have years of experience and the benefit of mentors with training and knowledge, not only in the field of herbalism but in the medical field. More than once an untrained dabbler in the herbals arts has landed themselves in the emergency room because they didn't know enough to realize that even handling some of these herbs fresh can cause poisoning.

If you are looking for one of these ointments or you are thinking of experimenting with some of these toxic herbs, then I suggest you examine you motives. Life is far too precious to risk on such pursuits and few who pursue it have the knowledge or the discipline to do so with any amount of safety. Do not risk your health or life for such frivolous pursuits. If what you seek is a spiritual or even a magickal experience, there are lots of techniques and practices that can be learned that are much safer.

Dragon's Blood

A Raven's Flight Phenomena

You might be wondering why I have dedicated a whole chapter, albeit a short one, to Dragon's Blood, since there are no other chapters dedicated to a single botanical substance. You might also be wondering why I consider it to be a "Raven's Flight Phenomena". What follows is a little bit of history and a little bit of lore that I hope helps to illustrate a little bit about Raven's Flight.

Natural Dragon's Blood (Daemonorops draco) is a very hard, very deep red resin that comes from a tree primarily grown in Sumatra. This resin has found many commercial uses over the years but it also occupies a very important niche in the magickal world. Magickally speaking, Dragon's Blood is very powerful all by itself, but it is also a very powerful ingredient when blended with others. Some of its many magickal associations are passion, power, success and strength. It also is closely associated with the planetary energies of Mars and the mythical energies of the Dragon. It is also used extensively to pump-up the power of the other ingredients. Kind of like magickal steroids, but without any nasty side effects.

Raven's Flight was once a real live brick and mortar store and from the beginning I always sold herbs, oils and a few of my own formulations. As the demand for my magickal products grew, so did my need and desire for ingredients. One of my favorite ingredients had long been Dragon's Blood resin, but I was only able to add it to charcoal burning incense and magickal candles. This was due to the fact that the only form of Dragon's Blood I could acquire was the resin.

I wanted a natural Dragon's Blood oil in the worst way, but all that I could find were sweetly scented synthetic fragrance oils. I remember one in particular that smelled a lot like cherry cough syrup. No matter where I searched, I could not find an essential oil, or even a semi-natural oil of Dragon's Blood. While I am not completely opposed to synthetic fragrance oils, none of them felt right. The energy of the resin was simply nonexistent in the available oils. So, began my quest to make a real and true Dragon's Blood oil with all the associated magickal power and energy.

Before I was successful I had to learn all sorts of things about extraction processes and solubility and so on and so forth. In time, I was finally able to extract the essence of the resin into an oil that was not only viable and authentic in every way, but it also felt right and it smelled right, too. Quite frankly, it smells a bit like iron - like blood.

Okay, so I admit I'm a little weird, but I love the way my "Real Dragon's Blood" oil smells. I add only a very small amount of one other essential oil as a fixative, but other than that it is all Dragon's Blood and base oil. Due to popular demand though, I had to make a more universally pleasant smelling oil. It appears that not everyone likes the slightly metallic smell of blood, go figure! So again, after much trial and error, I came up with what is known today as "Double Dragon's Blood Oil" and so began what I like to call "the phenomena".

Once I used this oil to make stick incense, my business changed forever. My Dragon's Blood stick incense was an immediate hit. I could hardly keep up with the demand at my store and that was before I started selling it wholesale and online. Many were the times that friends, family and coven-mates were drafted for incense sorting, bagging, boxing and tagging.

In time, I refined the oil extraction process to keep up with the demand. Any magickal product I put the oil into became a great seller. Truth is, my Dragon's Blood products made it possible for the whole line of Raven's Flight magickal products to flourish. That is the phenomenal part about it. Staying true to its magickal energies, Dragon's Blood really helped to power the success of the Raven's Flight Magickal Apothecary line. Many of my best wholesale and retail customers came to me originally because of the Dragon's Blood line of magickal products. I have often joked that when I perfected that oil, my life became Dragon's Blood.

Still today, it is the most popular stick and cone incense, lotion, soap, oil, etc. It is also an important part of many of my other blends. For some, it would seem that the stick incense just borders on being addictive. I have many customers who wear the oil and/or lotion as their personal scent.

Truth is, this little story is not really about a phenomena. What it is really about is sound magickal theory in practice. My ultimate intention was to have a successful magickal products business. The immediate need was to create the oil that would be the tool of that success. My actions, focused by the desire, combined with the inherent energy of Dragon's Blood to create just the reality that it was my intention to create. See, magick does work! Of course, it always helps when you apply a little elbow grease.

Recommended Reading List

Spell Books

There are literally 100s of spell books in publication today. There are only a few that have been around long enough to be considered classics. If they've been around for years you can be reasonably sure that they are worth having or at least reading. There are new spell books being published all the time and few are groundbreaking, extraordinary or even memorable. Most of them will not have the legs to still be in publication in 10, 5 or even 3 years. Having said that, there are also very few are truly awful.

I collected spell books for many years, then a few years ago I divested myself of most of them. Not because they were bad, but just because I no longer needed them. You kind-of out grow them after a while. Of course, I didn't get rid of all of them. I did keep the ones that were different, interesting or extremely well written.

I have listed what I feel are a few good spell books. If a book is not listed it certainly doesn't mean that it's not a good or decent spell book. It's just that for the reasons I've already given there is just no use in listing them all and quite simply there is not enough room. The books listed are but a small sampling of the available spell books that I feel are actually worth having.

Spell and How They Work by Janet & Stewart Farrar
A good basic book on the mechanics and philosophy of spell crafting. Definitely a classic in the genre.

Good Magic by Marina Medici
An excellent book for the beginning spell crafter. Informative and positive.

Charms, Spells and Formulas by Ray Marlborough
A classic down and dirty spell book heavily influenced by Hoodoo[26].

Spell Crafts by Scott Cunningham
This book is full of very homey, handicraft types of projects. I like it because it illustrates how many everyday crafts can be magickal crafting tools.

A Century of Spells by Draja Mickaharic
Spells influenced by many different cultures and perspectives.

Everyday Magic by Dorothy Morrison
Okay, I have to admit that I am a personal fan of the author. She is frank, honest, and ethical and has a great laugh. On top of all of that, she writes very well crafted books including a few spell books like this one. I may not always agree with her point of view but I always respect it.

Reference Books

Most of the reference books I have listed are by Scott Cunningham. There is good reason for this. Cunningham wrote good reference books. It's not that the information isn't available elsewhere, because it is. Cunningham was simply wise enough to gather it all up and put together

---

26   *Hoodoo is a truly American type of folk magick that evolved mostly from the traditions of the African-American slaves but was also influenced by Native American lore and tradition as well as some European practices.*

in fairly comprehensive collections of information and lore on various topics. These books are not exhaustive though and the serious crafter will eventually outgrow them but never actually throw them away.

Complete Book of Incense, Oils and Brews by Scott Cunningham

I have mixed feelings about this book. On one hand the table of correspondences is great. All of Cunningham's tables of correspondences are great, especially for the beginner. On the other hand, for the most part I think his recipes leave a lot to be desired. While they are all correct magickally, in my opinion they do not meet the other important criteria for a quality magickal product......most of them don't smell very good. Of course, that's just this crafter's opinion.

Cunningham's Encyclopedia of Magical Herbs by Scott Cunningham

Almost any magickal encyclopedia of magickal herbs is worth having and this is pretty much the standard for most spell crafters. My copy has been around for many, many years and is worn almost beyond being usable.

Cunningham's Encyclopedia of Crystal, Gem and Metal Magic by Scott Cunningham

A very easy to use reference book for working with stones and metals. Not the most comprehensive book on the subject but a great place to start.

Hoodoo Herb and Root Magic: A Materia Magica of African-American Conjure by Catherine Yronwode

Not a book for everyone, but a great resource for those who are interested in this truly American and very un-Wiccan type of magic.

Recommended Sources for Magickal Products

First off, let's get the shameless self-promotion out of the way. You can find my products online and direct at: www.ravensflight.net.

I am not going to pretend that the following list of metaphysical/pagan shops is an exhaustive one but it is a list of the shops that currently carry my products as well as other good products. Since I am of the firm belief that my products are good quality magickal products I can safely say that the shops listed can if fact, be recommended as good sources for good quality magickal products.

Some of the shops have web sites and some do not. All but one of the shops listed is an actual store where you can go in and shop.

Cauldron

2818 Rowena Ave.
Los Angeles, CA 90027
323-644-0268
http://www.cauldronkitty.com/

Enchanted Crystal

31982 Hilltop Blvd.
Running Springs, CA 92382
909-867-1190
enchcrystal@earthlink.net
(*Special note-Raven's Flight Products are sold here but under the name
"Enchanted Mountain". It's a long story....)

Enchanted Cottage

316 H St
Bakersfield, CA 93304
661-323-9929
valynncottage@sbcglobal.net

Celebration Conscious Living Store

2209 West Colorado Ave
Colorado Springs, CO 80904
719-634-1855
celebrationstore@comcast.net

Lady of the Lake-Temecula

27326 Jefferson St. Ste#19
Temecula, CA 92590
619-281-7231

Lady of the Lake-San Diego

3102 University Ave.
San Diego, CA 92104
909-260-4757

Lady of the Lake-Vista

20 Main St. Ste. #120
Vista, CA 92083
951-296-0222

Lady of the Lake-Idyllwild

54225 N. Circle Dr. #12
Idyllwild, CA 92549
951-659-5115

Odyssey

25 East Potomac St
Williamsport, MD 21795
301-223-8900

For Mystic Mind

2841 N. Green Valley Parkway
Henderson, NV 89014
702-434-7626

Gargoyle's

4550 University Way NE
Seattle, WA 98105
206-632-4940

Circle of the Green Fairy

5619 Hwy 42
Hattiesburg, MS 39401
601-583-1918
greenfaery@msn.com

Magical Senses

560 N Citrus Ave
Crystal River, FL 34428
352-795-9994

Mystical Fire

40879 Hwy 41, Ste#1A
Oakhurst, CA 93644
559-658-5900

The Mystic Merchant

1640 Copenhagen Drive
Solvang, CA 93463
805-693-1424
mysticmerchantsolvang.com

Raven's Loft

www.ravensloft.biz

Stonehenge

180 High Street
Harpers Ferry, WV 25425
304-535-1971

Other Manufacturers that I Recommend

I am sure that there are many fine and ethical formulators of magickal products that are available for sale but alas I know only a few. This is do to the fact that 98.275% of the time, I use my own products.

Moonlight Cove- You would think that since I make oils that I would make all of my own oils. Well, that is almost true. There is only one other formulator's oil that I wear and her name is Hillary and she is the formulator and owner of Moonlight Cove.
stores.ebay.com/Moonlight-Cove-Magick-Apothecary

Mermade Magickal Arts-Owned and operated by Katlyn Breene. Mermade Magickal Arts makes a fine selection of oils but the real quality product in my opinion is the charcoal incense. These products are fairly

hard to find but a few choice stores do carry them. There is a web address, but as of this writing the site is not yet functional. The company is based in Las Vegas, Nevada.
www.mermadearts.com

Star Child Incense- This company, based out of England has a full line of magickal products but I can really on comment on their charcoal incense. Based on the recommendation of very good friend I carried these in my store for a while and they truly are excellent. Almost as good as mine even if they are a little pricey.
starchild-international.com.

Coventry Creations- Manufacturers of the Blessed Herbal Candle line. I used to sell these candles in my store and I've burned a few over the years. Good candles. Now they have a whole line of products. The products are available in stores or check out their web site.
www.coventrycreations.com

Daughters of Isis- These products come highly recommended by a crafter I know and trust.
www.ancestoraromachologie.com

Just for Fun

These are products that are formulated with magickal flair but they aren't actually what I would call *serious* magickal products. They are fun though and we all need a little fun in our lives.

Witchy Poo - Lotions, potions and even cosmetics. Available in select stores and online.
www.witchypoobath.com

Mermaid's Bath-All sorts of wonderful bath products made by a lovely lady.
http://www.mermaidsbath.com/

Index

www.ingramcontent.com/pod-product-compliance
Lightning Source LLC
Chambersburg PA
CBHW051816040426
42446CB00007B/693